This was a grade.

Khrushchev makes the magic happen.

Edited by Jake Wilson

FOR MR. SMITH

TABLE OF CONTENTS

TABLE OF CONTENTS

TABLE OF CONTENTS

jake
WILSON
An Introduction

Remember *Choose Your Own Adventures*?

Imagine a book that functions like a multiple choice test. At the end of almost every page, the reader was presented with options. Throw the golden fish back? Turn to page 273. Ask the fish its name on a lark? Turn to page 95. The story changes based on the decisions of the reader, giving young readers a chance to be a part of the experience, albeit in a very limited way. These books plagued me for two reasons - I had to read every possible outcome, and I never agreed with the options presented. Why couldn't I just keep the fish?

This type of entertainment still exists, and I still get frustrated in the same ways. Video games now present vast worlds of opportunities for players to explore, but the story inevitably breaks at a decision between saving the innocents or sacrificing them. Sneaking by the dozing sentry or destroying his truck in a massive explosion. No matter how you look at it, it's a choice between A or B, and C just isn't even an option.

When it is, it isn't always helpful. Anyone who has been a student in the last 25 years has taken and hated a standardized test. These types of English tests have always been the worst. Interpret this poem, but limit yourself to these four options. Ignore your instincts, your history, your humanity. Ignore your knowledge of the poet or the greater context of society at the time of composition. Ignore the nuance of the written word. Look at these four options, and choose the "right" interpretation.

It's no wonder that writing is such a challenge. There are infinite possibilities, and that's just in constructing a single sentence. The word *the* can be followed by a plethora of nouns and adjectives, and every single one opens a different door. A story that starts with "The man" is drastically different than the one that starts with "The boy" or "The child" or even "The girl." That's assuming, of course, that the author wants to follow the protocols laid out hundreds of years ago. Writing about "the girl" is worlds apart from describing "The Girl."

And that's a *very* different tale than one featuring "The Man."

Every letter of every word is a decision, and it can't be broken down into four choices, much less two. In a world where students are constantly bombarded with straightforward and limited decisions in both their academic and entertainment lives, this can be intimidating. It can be tempting to avoid such work in the hopes it will go away and be replaced with the safer world of black and white, right and wrong. A or B. With an essay or a story, some may like it and others may not, whereas with multiple choice, you're either right or wrong. It's just a simpler space.

The writers in the following pages did not choose that simpler space. Some may have preferred it in the beginning of our time together, but it wasn't long before they stepped up to the challenge. Each author in this book has written more than 30 papers in the last several months. That's thirty questions answered, thirty experiences captured, thirty ideas put into hundreds of words, making for more than thirty million choices made by each and every of the 72 authors in this book.

And now you have a choice to make. Where will you start and where will you go? It's not as easy as choosing between releasing the fish or talking to it. You have to choose between 72 different stories, each one featuring infinite choices. The nice part is that each of *those* choices is made for you.

You just have to make the initial one - which story will you start with?

Once finished, which one will you read next?

I

ALLMAN
Charlotte's Adventure

The wariness had been apparent on Charlotte's face for two days now. She took notice of the two large and dark ships that had been following the Blistering Sun, the ship her family was travelling on. They were moving back to America, but only had a week or two left on their 4 week journey. She had mentioned the ships to her father, but he showed no signs of being concerned and tried to leave Charlotte with the reassurance that it was probably a group of merchant ships. Charlotte's family was the only other family on it, therefore she had made no acquaintances, unless you count the sailor who brings her books everyday from her trunk that's stored down below. Although Charlotte loved reading, the days she spent at sea seemed to drag on long and boring. Her thoughts were interrupted by a sudden tap on the shoulder. She turned around to be faced with a familiar sailor. He said nothing, but just simply pointed towards the entrance to the cabin area, Charlotte thought this was extremely unusual and even though she was unsure why she had to return to her cabin, she scurried off to her room.

The next morning, Charlotte was awoken by her mother telling her they were going to explore the island the boat had stopped at. Once they were there, she recognized the ships that had been following them were at the port as well. The ships names were scratched off, so you could barely read what they said, but she could recognize the look of the ships very easily. It still bothered her that the adults chose to neglect the situation. After being on the island for two hours, Charlotte started to feel nauseous so she went back to the ship to take a nap. Her mother said they would return to the ship later in the evening and suggested that Charlotte go ahead and eat dinner without them. She returned to the ship and quickly ate her dinner then went straight to her cabin and fell asleep. She woke up surrounded in darkness; however, she realized it wasn't her room. Apprehension grew as terrifying possibilities ran through her mind as to why she was in this dingy room. The door was shut and locked, showing no signs of her being able to escape. Charlotte was so terrified all she could do was sit and stare at the wall. Just as she started to doze off, she jumped to her feet, startled, as the door flew open.

"Come with me," demanded the strange man with dark hair and tan skin. Realizing it was smart to show no reluctance, Charlotte obediently followed him. He took her to what looked like a makeshift kitchen and served her stale crackers with water. Then, she was taken back to the tiny room. This routine occurred for what Charlotte assumed was a week, she had been trying to keep up with how many nights had passed but she lost count. She had noticed large containers which she assumed were some kinds of goods, and the ship had very few sailors. This opened up an opportunity for her to make a casual, or nonviolent, escape. Charlotte had begun to notice how hot the small and damp room was, now regretting wearing so many layers . She considered removing one, but was worried she would get cold in the middle of the night, so she kept on her multiple layers and suffered through the heat.

Around two days later, Charlotte woke up to hear calls of seagulls which meant they were at a port. Considering she had been on a ship before, she slowly started to recognize more distinct noises as she woke up. She could only hope the few sailors were unloading on the dock so she could escape. Up until this point, they hadn't stopped at any ports and she realized her first chance to escape might be her only chance. She hurried to get off the ground and developed a plan. Believing the circumstance of her having to escape excused it, she tore off her top layer skirt allowing her to move freely in her thin layered skirt. Charlotte noticed a small but heavy crate over in the corner of her room and quickly went over to pick it up. She dropped the crate onto the door handle causing the handle to no longer be intact. She then sprinted to the top deck and quickly noticed the left loading ramp was busy with sailors so she dashed down the right side ramp. Luckily, she was hidden in the considerable amount of people walking on the dock. As Charlotte quickly stumbled and pushed her way through the crowd, she tripped and fell into a very familiar person. She had no intention of crying, but she couldn't contain her feelings of relief when she saw it was her cousin Anthony.

"Anthony, what are you doing here?" Charlotte asked. He quickly embraced her and then explained that when her family realized she had been kidnapped, an investigation was opened. As soon as they discovered she had been kidnapped by pirates who wanted ransom money, they used shipping records to pinpoint the ship's next stop to this port. Anthony had been the first one to volunteer to come down and retrieve Charlotte. He informed her that the family was awaiting her arrival at a big house they were renting not far from the port. With the convenience of her family's rental carriage, Anthony and Charlotte left the port and were able to arrive at the house within thirty minutes. Once she set foot in the parlor at the house, relatives showered her with affection. Later that night, Charlotte sat on her balcony watching ships sail in and out of port. Once she was in bed, she stayed up letting her mind wander to thoughts on her experience and temporary life at sea. Charlotte knew that the nightmares of her terrible experience would haunt her for a while, and she would live with that small fear of her kidnappers roaming free, but she knew she was now safe with her family.

carley
ALMARAZ
Who Stole the Library Pass?

Recently, the eighth grade library pass for Mr. Wilson's class had gone missing, and no one knows whom to suspect. This is important because the 8th grade classes of Mr. Wilson need to go to the library to help with their assignment of having to read two books every month. Mr. Wilson also believes that they are responsible for what they lose, and because of this he will not give his classes a new library pass. Seeing as this is an issue, they have called me to help with the situation and hopefully find the pass. With the help of my team of investigators from my company, We Will Solve It, I am hoping to get to the bottom of it to not only promote my business of investigation, but to help the kids. I have recently gotten footage from the library to see which students were in the library; three students came up: Greg Smith in 1st block, Louis Marson in 2nd block, and Christina Martin in 3rd block. These three students were each representing their class periods and bringing Ms. Harrison, the librarian, their class fines that day while carrying the library pass around.

"Good Morning, students! My name is Brenda Marshall, and I am here to interrogate you three and some staff to solve the issue of who stole the library pass. The three of you seem to be the three eighth graders who are most seen with the pass in the footage we have, so I would like to ask you each a few questions," I said to the eighth graders. They all agreed with a casual head nod, seeing as they wanted the library pass back too, so I continued with precise instructions on how to proceed. I first summoned Greg Smith into the counselor's office, and he began his story.

I asked him to state his whole story and to not leave any details out. He started with his shower and breakfast, sardonically going step by step through his day. It was all irrelevant, but then I actually started to pay attention when he said, "...then I walked into Mr. Wilson's class." Greg explained the brief lesson given by Mr. Wilson when Mr. Wilson interrupted himself. His voice pervaded the classroom. "Smith, please take the library fines to Ms. Harrison and be back in 5 minutes." Greg said that he grabbed the pass and headed in the halls toward the library where he then set it down. After he handed Ms. Harrison the money, he quietly left with the pass in hand. Greg headed straight back to Wilson's class, where he put the pass back on the wall and went to his seat.

After I heard Greg's story, I realized it was impossible for Louis to have done anything, seeing he was second block and the block after that had the pass, so I decided to send Louis back to class and consult with Christina next.

Christina started off confidently, as if there was no chance she could ever lose something. In summary, she had started her story off the same way Greg had with what was happening in Mr. Wilson's class and the way he told her to take care of the fines. Christina then grabbed the pass and started towards the door. While explaining her walk in the hall, she told me she was one of those forgetful people that overlooks everything. She wasn't hesitant to remember that she walked down the hall, took care of fines, and then got distracted by the art teacher wanting her to look at some artwork because she was "very talented," (as she told me). She told me she doesn't remember the rest, but was pretty sure she didn't have it when she went back to class. She looked in awe as if she would have never thought she could have lost the pass, but it didn't matter: I needed to move on with the case.

I hastened to the art teacher's room and asked if she had seen the library pass. She then told me, "No, but Mr. Wilson did come in here, picked up some paper, and then left."

Straight after that conversation, I went back to Mr. Wilson's classroom and asked Mr. Wilson about what I had just discovered, and he said that he had just taken some write ups since he was in the 7th grade hallway and needed some. He looked confused as to why I would ask that question, so I concisely explained what had happened, and then I went back to the counselor's office. With no other suspects, I wearily closed my case and headed for the doors to leave Madison Eagles Middle School. I had gotten nowhere today. What should I do next? As I was going through my day all over again to see if I overlooked anything, I remembered an earlier conversation with Ms. Harrison about what she had done that day. She had said to me that she had went to the art room herself with Mr. Wilson and grabbed a stack of papers next to him. That was when I remembered seeing a paper with students handwriting written all over it on top of her desk, so I now had to propose my next speculation: did Ms. Harrison accidentally steal the pass?

I immediately ran to the library where I hoped to find Ms. Harrison. I walked in and was surprised to find her actually shredding the pass. I hastily ran over to where she was, but when I got there, it was too late, and the pass was gone forever. I called my team of investigators over to come and interrogate her while I informed Mr. Wilson of the news. When I told Mr. Wilson who it was, he was in bewilderment, seeing as he and Ms. Harrison were good friends. We were also shocked to hear that Ms. Harrison did this entire thing just so at the end of the year she could sell all the books the students didn't buy and get rich off of the entire thing. The children were appalled when they heard the news, but some relief was lifted when Mr. Wilson explained that they would get another pass, free of charge.

My team and I had left with our heads held high, with a good review of how well we worked on this case written by the school's principal at Madison Eagles Middle School, and now we were ready to take on another case.

W
AREVALO

As Summer stared back at her reflection, she sighed. Her hair was a tangled mess. Her once austere locks were now bunched up amongst each other. She guessed it was time to pull out her hat. It was a black beanie - her favorite. She slid it over her head and checked her appearance. It was much better than her original bed-head hair.

Summer went to the kitchen, goaded out of her room by the tantalizing smell of maple syrup and melted chocolate, and sat down. Her mother, Natalia, turned away from the stove and brought a steaming pile of chocolate chip pancakes to Summer. As she put them down in front of her daughter, Natalia stared at Summer's hat.

"What are you, some kind of emu?" she asked, laughing a bit.

"What?" Summer replied, concentrating on pouring the perfect amount of syrup on her pancakes.

"Your hat. You look like an emu." Natalia was still smiling ridiculously.

She means emo, Summer thought.

"Yeah, mom, I'm totally an emu," Summer said jokingly, rolling her eyes. Natalia shrugged and went back to the stove. Summer laughed under her breath.

An emu? Right.

Finally, Summer took a bite of her pancakes, enjoying the sticky-sweet flavor of the melted chocolate mixing with the maple syrup. As the savory scents of the sugary breakfast trickled down her throat, Summer spontaneously felt very sick. She staggered to her feet, groaning at the wrenching pain that had appeared in her lower abdomen. Reassuring her mother that she was alright, Summer stumbled to the bathroom and leaned over the sink. A frantic knock came at the door.

"Is everything okay?" Natalia inquired.

Summer looked up into the mirror

"Yeah, mom I-" Summer cut herself off. Feathers. Feathers were growing where her hair should've been. In fact, they were growing all over her body. Summer held her hands in front of her face, but instead of her normally pale arms, she now saw many-feathered wings. Summer let out a gasp and looked down. Her legs were skinny and grey, and her feet had turned to talons. Summer staggered backwards and looked into the mirror again.

A bird? she thought, a little more than disconcerted. *No, an emu...what could've done this to me? Maybe it was the pancakes...*

10

Summer attempted to open the door with her new wings, but to no avail. Her feathers kept on slipping off of the doorknob. Natalia was also pounding away at the other side, franticly trying to get to her daughter and making the door shake.

"Summer? Summer, are you alright?"

"Uh...yeah. Could you open the door for me?" Summer replied, relieved she still sounded like herself.

As Natalia opened the door, Summer winced.

What is mom going to say?

Expecting the worst, Summer readied herself for a panicked, worried mother. However, when the bathroom door was completely opened, Natalia simply looked Summer up and down very calmly. Her eyes widened, and Natalia began shaking with derisive laughter.

"I-I knew you were an emu!" she gasped out.

Summer glared at her mother until, at last, her peals of laughter died down.

"I-I'm sorry, Summer. I didn't mean to laugh so much at your...predicament," Natalia apologized, though she was still smirking.

"Yeah, sure you are," Summer shot back, the pain in her stomach now gone.

"No, really. I am. Maybe I can find a way to help you fix this," Natalia said sincerely as she guided Summer out of the bathroom.

*   *   *

After a few weeks had passed, Summer was getting used to being an emu. She was used to being home-schooled and to eating differently. She was used to her large wings making it difficult to walk through doors. And she was used to being stuck inside, where she'd be hidden from the public. She missed her old life, but she was quickly realizing that she *liked* being an emu. It allowed her to be grumpy and bad-tempered without Natalia thinking she was being disrespectful or incredulous. She ate more healthily than she used to, and being an emu gave her an excuse to get people to open doors for her (though the only person she was around was Natalia). Summer decided to tell her mother all of these things when she had a chance. Summer had decided to stay an emu.

"Summer! Summer, wake up! I found a way to fix you!" Natalia exclaimed.

Summer had fallen asleep while thinking about how she would tell her mother how she truly felt, and Natalia was now shaking her awake.

"All you need is a baby's foot, some olive oil, and the eggshell of a newly-hatched emu...do you think you could lay any eggs? Well, we'll get to that later...

THIS WAS A GRADE.

Anyway, you just cook them all together at two-hundred and fifty degrees for fifteen minutes and chant - hold on and let me find it-

'Restore me to the way I was

Without the feathers, fluff, and fuzz,'

until you're a regular human being again! Aren't you so glad?" Natalia rambled, throwing the book she was reading from to the side.

"Of course, it will be difficult, you have to…"

Summer had awakened somewhere near the middle of this, and, at this point, she was tired of her mother trying to 'fix her.' So, Summer put a feathered wing to her mother's lips, silencing her. Summer leaned in towards her mother, her face getting more sincere with every breath. At last, when her beak was mere centimeters from Natalia's face, she whispered one thing, and one thing only.

"This isn't a phase, mom. This is who I really am."

gabby
ATKINSON
Remember This

Elanoir didn't know where she was. She woke up in a chair next to a tall house on a very green lawn. Since the last thing she remembered was getting into the car with her husband after their wedding reception, terror struck her. She was no longer dressed in her wedding gown, but clad in a white shirt and navy blue slacks. She felt tired and frail, so frail that she felt if someone were to gently touch her arm, she would topple over. Not bothering to look around or yell for help, for she was so scared, she immediately hurried away from the house.

She moved out onto the driveway and into the road. She stopped a jogging man and asked what town she was in. He replied with, "Sikeston, Missouri, Ma'am," giving her a weird look and continued on.

Elanoir was relieved to know that she was still in her home town. Weaving her way through back roads very slowly and painfully, while occasionally stopping and asking for directions, she finally made her way to to her destination: Woodington Park.

Woodington Park was the last place she remembered because it was where she got married. Ignoring her aching bones and muscles, she passed through the iron gates that protected the park. While she was walking she was too panicked to notice her surroundings, but now as she looked up she saw how different things were. The town had added more benches, trees, and lamps. She also noticed how different the clothing was. They were brighter and had different patterns on them. Her wedding decorations were gone and so were her guests. She saw children running around, a couple picnicking, a man playing Frisbee with his dog, and an older couple taking a walk. She smiled at the last people. She wants her and her husband to grow old together, only now she couldn't find him.

Irving Vancouver was the man who stole her heart. This beautiful man had so rudely intruded on her overly privileged life. She could perfectly remember that her first look at him had been dismissive. It was only when he asked her to dance did she notice his charm. While they danced and talked at a charity banquet, she couldn't help but feel an apparent affection growing between them. Friends and family anticipated their inevitable engagement. They were married three months after their engagement party.

At their wedding in the back of Woodington Park, Irving pulled her aside into an orchard of trees, to carve their initials in the biggest one. It was these silly, but cheesy things that had made her fall madly in love with him. Like when they watched the sunset together on her birthday one year.

After walking to the back of the park, Elanoir finally found the orchard. She located the familiar giant apple tree, with delicious, ripe apples that bloom in the spring, in the middle, that had a new bench underneath it. Moving around to its back she ran her fingers over the little heart that said, "IV+EV." Tears sprang to her eyes as she looked at them, savoring the feelings of love they restored. Oh how she wished Irving was right there with her. She missed his wavy blond hair and cornflower blue eyes. She just wished she could find him so she could see that cute dimpled smile he always had on his face.

"Mom?" a soft, hesitant voice interrupted her wishful thinking. She turned to see a stunning woman. Why, she could be Irving's daughter! All the way from the cornflower blue eyes and blond hair to the dimpled smile.

Full of confusion and awe, she warily stated, "No dear. I am not your mother. I'm too young. Though you do look an awful lot like my husband, he is also too young to be your father."

The beautiful woman sighed and sat down on the bench. Beckoning Elanoir over, the woman reached down and pulled out of her jeans what looked like a small mirror box. When she noticed Elanoir's hesitation she sighed and handed it to her saying, "Here: use my phone to see your reflection. Where do I begin? Okay my name is Adelaide Vancouver James, daughter of Irving Elanoir, you, Vancouver. I am thirty-five, married, and with two children of my own, Ellie and Irik, after you and dad.

"Now would be the time for you to look because you won't believe me otherwise."

Elanoir brought the box, or 'phone,' to her face and gasped. Staring back at her was an elderly woman with bright green eyes. Wrinkles adorned her forehead and mouth, and her hair was in a white-silver bob. Looking down she now noticed how her body had changed. She was shorter and her skin had aged. How had she lost all those years? This must be a joke!

"Mom, you have Alzheimer's. You were diagnosed two years ago. You are now sixty-four years old." Adelaide took a deep breath, her explanation concise, and continued, "Mom...Dad passed away last year from a heart attack." Her words hit Elanoir like a freight train, knocking her right off course.

Elanoir looked deep into the eyes of the woman sitting in front of her. She contemplated the idea of her being her child. All she saw was truth and honesty; Elanoir believed her. Taking a shaky breath, she sat down next to Adelaide. So why did she all of a sudden remember her wedding? Why was she remembering anything at all? And then she realized she knew exactly why. Irving was giving her one last chance to tell her daughter what she needed to.

"Okay."

"Okay? You'll come back to the retirement home with me?" her daughter asked.

"Yes I will. But first," she gently took Adelaide's hands in hers and held them tightly, "I have to tell you something."

"Yes?"

"Even though I won't remember you, no matter what, remember this: I'll always love you," and she pulled her now crying daughter into her arms, hugging her for the little time they had left before her memory drifted into confusion once again.

joshua
BAHN
Skydiving

Jake rolled over in his bed to turn off his alarm clock, which went off at 6:00 in the morning. He roused himself from the bed and got in the shower to restore his unkempt hair to its customary spiked-up position. After finishing the rest of his morning routine, that consisted of breakfast, and brushing his teeth, Jake headed to his school, Field High School. His first two classes, English and science, went relatively smoothly, but in history, things were not as good.

Dylan, one of Jake's acquaintances in his history class, approached him with a strange looking object which was confined in a box. In fact, the item inside the box was a magic eight ball, which they tried playing with before class but was cut off when the bell rang. After class was out, Jake asked the ball, "What does my near future hold?"

It responded, "Your death is imminent."

Dylan, however, also asked the same question and received a better fortune which said, "In algebra, you will make a 100 on your test."

Jake was startled by this, and thought that it wasn't fair that Dylan would get a good grade, but reassured himself that the ball was just a stupid toy. After that day, Jake was scheduled to go to Dylan's birthday party with some of his other friends from school.

At the party, which was quite boring, Jake proposed that they play truth or dare in an effort to liven up the atmosphere. Over the course of the game, several truths and dares were issued, like having to go knock on the neighbor's door and run or to wear something ridiculous to school, but Jake's turn was still yet to come. Finally, it was his turn, and he chose a dare because he did not want to have to reveal anything embarrassing about himself in the instance that he chose truth. He was apprehensive about this decision, recalling the fortune he had received earlier and did not want to have to do anything dangerous that risked his life.

Alas, Jake received his dare from his friends, and it left him appalled. The teens had given him two options: to wrestle a crocodile or to go skydiving along with his friends. After meditating on and contemplating his decision, Jake chose skydiving over the crocodile because he was extremely afraid of their massive bodies and razor sharp rows of teeth. The date was set to go skydiving with his friends the next day. Although his outlook seemed grim, he was not going to disappoint. For the rest of the party, the teens continued with the game, most of them enjoying the opportunity to socialize. However, Jake was no longer having an enjoyable time; he was more worried about how he was going to be subjected to skydiving the next day.

The next day, his alarm clock went off at 6:00 AM, which meant the start to an day that looked bleak in Jake's mind. Although scared, he put the silly fortune into the back of his mind in an effort to forget about it. After driving to the launch site, the group was soon four thousand feet up and preparing to jump. The only person who was nervous was Jake, because everyone besides him had been skydiving before when they were in Hawaii for a vacation.

"Everyone check your parachutes! After about one minute of freefall, I want you to pull the cord on your left to deploy the parachute! If you do this, all should go as planned, but if not, there is a backup parachute cord on your right side! Only pull this cord in an emergency! Get ready...Jump!" The pilot had to shout because of the sound of the engine and wind made it hard to hear.

Jake winced as he took the first step out of the plane and was immediately terrified, though he slightly enjoyed the experience. Jake liked the rush of cool air streaming around his body, and to him, it felt like he was flying, even though he was actually falling. Then after about a minute, Jake reached to his left to pull the cord. However, the stitching had come undone and the cord ripped off, not pulling the parachute with it. Everyone else's cord fully opened the parachute, but Jake kept descending.

He was going mad with fear. He thought about the eight ball's prediction and regretted coming in the first place because now he believed he was going to die. With almost all hope gone, Jake remembered to pull the backup parachute cord, which opened fully and slowed his falling speed. Jake was relieved beyond imagination, because he truly believed that he was not going to survive.

Gliding to a slow stop on the desolate farmland, Jake was unharmed. Even though his legs were shaking from the encounter, he stood upright and walked to meet his friends. After talking about his experience, he declared he was never skydiving again because his life flashed before his eyes. Jake's friends said that they were scared for his life when they saw the time elapse before his parachute finally opened. Recovering from the near disaster, Jake got in his car and started on his way home. On the way, he overheard on the radio that there was a foot chase of a bank robber close to where Jake was. About five minutes later, he heard the faint reverberation of a police siren, and soon after, Jake had to stop for gas. While waiting outside of his car for the gas to pump, Jake saw the infamous bank robber running down the street towards him. Jake wanted to be a hero and started straight at the man to tackle him.

However, this gambit did not turn out the way Jake had planned, because, after making the initial contact with the robber, Jake fell directly to the ground. Infuriated, the robber, who was the bigger of the two men, picked Jake up and tossed him like a mere ragdoll in front of an oncoming bus. The magic eight ball's prediction was correct: Jake didn't survive.

autumn
BALE
The GoldenHam

"Extended-Fist-Bump-Partners, go!" shouted Mr. Wilson to his first period class who all turned to their assigned class partners. Becky Goldstein reluctantly turned to her Extended-Fist-Bump-Partner, Oliver Ham, or Hammy as he was popularly known. Hammy extended his fist to his Extended-Fist-Bump-Partner.

"Knuck me," he said to Goldstein. She refused to fist bump him due to the scorn she felt towards him. Instead, she only gave him a sardonic smile. She tried to not hate the one person she would be working with in class all year, but Hammy had made that difficult by constantly annoying her. The two were the "bestest friends in the whole wide world"...according to the seating chart. Hammy continued to pester her as she tried to work independently, and her lip trembled with rage...or was it passion?

Becky's friends, Robin and Summer exchanged glances and giggled at the two. The "GoldenHam", as they were called, had become the "ship," or pairing of the class. As the two were fangirling - which consisted of flailing, giggling and saying "omg they're so cute!" - Goldstein had become more agitated. Hammy always found new ways to upset her, whether it was stealing her paper or claiming her hard work. She hated it so much. Yet, somehow they knew deep down behind all the hatred, they had felt something a bit more for each other. Perhaps their relationship wasn't "intimate" as Hammy had once inappropriately used the vocabulary term, but there were certainly some feelings there.

Hammy, on the other hand, had confronted his feelings of love by joking about it - just like with the misused vocabulary incident. He would occasionally even flirt with her. For the most part, that's all the two were: a joke. Nothing more and nothing less.

The class had used this joke only in good fun. They would do things like make them read as Mary Russell and Sherlock Holmes or Romeo and Juliet and then laugh at how much Goldstein hated it and Hammy enjoyed it. They hadn't realized that the pair of Extended-Fist-Bump-Partners' feelings for each other had been very real. It was, after all, concealed by all the hatred and humor.

Goldstein stood at her locker which was crowded around by many people, including Hammy whose locker was next to hers. While sorting through her stuff, she had dropped one of her books. As if by fate, Hammy had accidentally dropped something too. Then the most cliché thing that ever existed in a love story happened. When they both reached down, their hands brushed against each other's. Goldstein started at his touch. "H-Hammy?" Goldstein stuttered.

Hammy decided to make his move. He leaned forward and kissed her cheek lightly. Goldstein was utterly confused. What had caused this erratic behaviour? Had he gone mad? She shut her locker and stood, giving him a quizzical look as she did so.

Before she could storm off down the hallway, Hammy took her hand. Except this time, she didn't object or pull away. Conveniently, no one had seen them except for Summer and Robin who were shocked by this revelation. Goldstein and Hammy smiled at each other. The pair of Extended-Fist-Bump-Partners knew it was meant to be.

After the couple somehow managed to endure five rough years of Hammy's cheesy jokes and Goldstein's wrath, Hammy had proposed to Goldstein who had finally said yes after a month of giving it some thought. Now Hammy stood at the altar waiting for the other half of the GoldenHam to walk down the aisle. When he first saw her, his heart skipped a beat. She walked down the aisle, clad in a white lace dress, a pair of black Converse, and her bracelets. Walking down the aisle was like walking through the hallway on the first day of school. It seemed as if everyone's eyes were on her which, in this case, they were.

Upon reaching the altar, Goldstein was able to register what Hammy was wearing: a khaki and neon tux. She internally cringed at the sight. She wondered how many times she would have to tell him to stop wearing that color combination - especially on their wedding day. She ignored it anyways, figuring it was his way to playfully agitate her which was how he usually expressed his love for her and greeted him with a warm smile.

"Do you take Becky Goldstein to be your lawfully wedded wife? Not that I'm sharing my beliefs or you're sharing yours.." said the officiant, Mr. Wilson, who was only there because the pair has managed to bribe him with a large amount of free comic books and green pens.

"I certainly do, coach," replied Hammy cheerfully.

"Do you take Oliver Ham to be your lawfully wedded husband?" he asked Goldstein.

"Yeah I guess.." she replied with a soft chuckle as she smiled at Hammy.

They slipped on their gold wedding bands which had been engraved with a Ham in front of a Nike symbol since Hammy wore Nike so much. The rings would bind them together forever. The rings would become precious.

"You may now fist-bump the bride," said Mr. Wilson. Hammy extended his fist to his wife who fist-bumped him back. It was a fist-bump of true love. Church bells rang and the audience, which mainly consisted of family members and classmates including Robin and Summer, cheered.

"Hey Goldstein. I like you," stated Hammy once the two were left alone, lingering at the altar.

Goldstein looked at him and blankly replied, "Oh really? I hadn't noticed."

"No, no! I *like-like* you," he replied.

"It's been literally five minutes and I am already 100% done with you. DIVORCE," she said. Her scowl broke out into a grin as she chuckled. She couldn't stay mad at him - even though she seemed like it when he pestered her so much. She remembered when Hammy decided to make a move on her and kissed her cheek so many years ago.

She gazed lovingly into his eyes which twinkled like stars in the sky as she replied, "I *like-like* you too."

Together, the GoldenHam literally skipped off into the sunset and burned to death.

a
BATEY
The Mug

I tried to shake off the fatigue of sitting through my language arts class. I wanted to succumb to sleep, but I knew I would have had to endure agonizing labor assigned to me by my teacher, Mr. Wilbert, if I did. I shivered as excruciating memories of writing my name hundreds of times, scrubbing the dingy floors, and being demeaned by my whole class resurfaced. I was deprived of sleep every night just because I was so desperate to complete my English homework. I was quietly fluctuating between consciousness and unconsciousness when the bell rang.

"Alright, ladies and gentlemen, I have to pick up your homework for tonight from the library. I suppose you can just talk or something, but if you get too loud, you know I will have to assign you extra work," Mr. Wilbert sighed and walked out of the door. Instead of staying in my seat as usual, I decided to get up and walk around so I could avoid my tiredness. I drifted over to the teacher's desk, overlooked the books and laid my eyes on his precious mug. He had won it from his favorite comic book convention, so it was decorated with characters from various television shows and limited edition comic books. I picked up the colorful object to examine the details when a group of turbulent students bumped into me, forcing my whole body into the wall. Immediately, I realized that the beloved mug had broken into roughly two pieces: the cup and the handle. Panic pervaded my whole body, and I began to rummage through all the drawers in the classroom looking for glue. The group of rambunctious peers had walked off, too interested in their conversation to notice me. Mr. Wilbert was still on his errand to receive the night's homework.

The whistling Mr. Wilbert could be heard at the end of the hall, and the students began to sit down, hoping to dodge trouble once the bell sounded for the second time. The teacher seemed to only be happy when he wasn't with us because we would often hear of fun activities he would do such as conventions and his lovely wife. Because of this attitude towards the class, I knew I would receive gruesome punishment, which impelled me to search faster. Finally, I found an industrial strength glue stick hidden under a few papers and I gingerly attached the handle back on the mug. I set the mug down where I found it and breathed out with relief when my peers were still chatting too much to notice what I was doing. I was hurrying back to my desk when Mr. Wilbert, back in his usual, poor disposition when he saw us, appeared at the door.

"Hey! Sit down unless you want me to triple the homework," he yelled at me. In my greatest attempt at being affable towards him, I forced a mellow smile and nodded. He started to move towards his desk as I did to mine, and we sat down at the same time. I began to shallow out my breathing and calm down. Mr. Wilbert began to pour himself a freshly brewed cup of coffee from his tiny convenience store brewer in the corner, and I was ecstatic to see that the glue was holding. I, in my usual seat, started to work on the assignment he had passed out at the beginning of class to occupy my time. I glanced back once more to see if the teacher had noticed, and saw that when he was preparing to take a sip, the handle snapped and the coffee mug dropped.

Coated in the scalding beverage, Mr. Wilbert's cry of exasperation was heard throughout the building. The class was startled by his reaction, and though some of them almost let a little giggle escape, most held their breath to avoid his wrath. I, trying to hide my guilt, turned around. That day we had all received detention, and though I eventually got over the whole thing, Mr. Wilbert never let up, always in a poor mood and shutting out the laughs he brought to other classes.

brazzle-
BRIZZLE
My Annabel

It was many and many years ago. She was barely 17, a flowering age, and I, 30. Many would not think that two people so unlike would ever even potentially fall in love. It was as if she was life, beautiful and endearing, and I death, dark and quiet, going mute in my own mind. But, we were puzzle pieces, so unlike that where I was empty, she filled me in, making my own soul whole. I never properly courted her, during the time women had been given a new found sense of freedom. I could not wait to marry her; we were both so full of anticipation. But, we were young. We were stupid.

Three years after our marriage she received the shocking news. It came about and tore my soul, that she had fixed, into pieces again, but she helped me. She told me not to fret; she would live. Oh, I was a fool for choosing to believe her, but love makes fools out of all of us. However, I enjoyed my remaining time with her, still choosing to be ignorant and ignore the fact that as my days seemed to prolong, hers seemed to shorten. The pain was too much to bear, and we were growing short of money, she was close to death, and it tantalized us both. But I did not let it show that I was also suffering. I would not let her spend the last years of her life believing it was her fault.

After almost five years with her burden of tuberculosis, she drifted away, and I cracked. Except, this time there was no one there to help me pick up the pieces. I had fallen into a melancholy, many times contemplating death.

People always told me to move on, but it hurt. Perhaps moving on would hurt less, but I could not abandon the only person who ever cared about me. I saw pieces of her in everyday life. Clothes and cups and more things, such as everyday household items, that she deserved to have longer, and soon I was forced to face the fact that I was the reason the gods chose to give it to her. They love to take things away from me, anyone I love eventually leaves, whether it is their will or not. They took my dear mother at my birth and my father soon after because he was so distraught, and they only reason being me. Me, me, me.

This is why she should not have loved me back. She should not have been so ignorant. But she was young. She was stupid. She was a fool for loving me, but love makes fools out of all of us.

I was drawn to her grave for the same reason I was drawn to her. Her soul made it full of color in an utterly dull world. She seemed to whisper to me as I lay by her, my wife. Her beauty had not left her. It continued like this for many and many months. I could always sense her presence; even death could not sever our bond of love. Being with her again was rejoicing; it filled me up to the brim, and pulled me together. Oh, the irony: the one so full of life before had gone cold. The broken one now whole. We were happy for a while. She would visit me every night, and when the wind blew, you could hear her whisper her deepest secrets to me.

However, like all good things, like all blissful lies in my life, my joy couldn't last. I believe it was late November, almost a year since I first took my midnight walk to where she so soundlessly slept, and crawled in with her. Someone had found me in her sepulcher, and they couldn't understand the eternal bond I had held with Annabel Lee. They had said I had gone mad, that I had finally taken the plunge into insanity. They wanted to take me away from my bride, but not before I got my chance to say goodbye. With my final words and my lips brushing against her bare forehead, I looked up to see her walking into the turbulent waves. As she walked away, she turned and didn't say anything, but I could tell what she meant by the way she affectionately stared at me.

When I was being dragged away, I knew what I had to do. Running towards the waves, I crashed in. My presence being a disruption like it had been the entirety of my life. Darkness was all I saw until she was there, pulling me up and out. And just like that, the cycle had come full circle.

aaron
BREWER
Heroes

I don't know what impelled me to come here tonight. Sitting on the fire escape and surveying the street below, tonight, I am a vigilante. My sister was killed by a lowlife in this city. It was a random act of violence, a robbery that escalated to murder. This is a story that happens all too often here. This city - *my* city - is like a festering, open wound. Like all infections, it needs a cure. I am that cure.

I'm clad in a black leather jacket with midnight blue gloves, black pants, black boots, a black ski mask, and over that, a white hockey mask. A staff is stationed on my back for close-quarter duels. It's not the best costume, but it conceals my identity and that's all I need it to do. My current appearance would probably instill fear in most scumbags, so it will work for now.

As I look down from the fire-escape, I see a group of four thugs. A fire burns bright in the trash can next to them. It looks like they're taking inventory of weapons and ammo. I can see the gleam of the weapons from all the way up here. They have pistols, semi-automatics, machetes, and switchblades. Pretty much the standard "starter package" for a criminal. They slowly pack the pistols away into their holsters. They are wearing an assortment of jackets and rolled up ski masks with fingerless gloves. My eyes casually go to my iPod as I search through the playlists. Bon Jovi, Guns n Roses, Queen it is! This is my first night on the job, but it doesn't mean I can't relish the fun of it. I run the ear buds beneath my ski mask and into my ears. The familiar song plays:

> Steve walks warily down the street
> The brim pulled way down low.
> And ain't no sound but the sound of his feet,
> Machine guns ready to go!

I climb down, jump off the end of the fire-escape, and land in front of the goons. My steel staff immediately releases from its position on my back. Initially, they are caught off guard, but they recover and begin their assault.

> Are you ready, hey, are you ready for this?
> Are you hanging on the edge of your seat?
> Out of the doorway the bullets rip!
> To the sound of the beat!

They pull out their guns and begin to fire. The bullets almost do go to the sound of the beat with their steady *rat-a-tat-tat*. I manage to pivot out of the way of the bullets. *They must be really bad shots*, I think. However, it seems that they are figuring out my technique. They are studying the way I move, the way I dodge, everything about my methods. They're not trying, just stalling.

Now the real danger starts! They forget the guns and go for their machetes. They're trying to get the drop on me. I guess they don't realize I've been training in hand to hand combat for quite a while. By now, I can take down a mugger with a blade easily. I manage to dodge the first attacker who fights in a blind rage. I grab his arm with both hands and twist as hard as I can to the right. He yelps in pain as the bone in his arm snaps. As I take him down, another chorus plays.

Another one bites the dust!
Another one bites the dust!
And another one gone and another one gone!
Another one bites the dust!

Another rushes towards me, but I duck and grab his legs, flipping him over me. Despite his apparent fear, the third one sprints forward, and I dance to the left, jump in the air, then reel around and kick him square in the nose. What can I say? These guys are no match for me. Though I've taken down these two, one more remains, and he looks like he's still thinking rationally.

His eyes examine me from head to toe, trying to figure out where the most damage can be inflicted. This will be interesting. He swings to the left and I parry to the right. He tries to go for my shoulder with a single swipe, but I manage to pivot out of the danger zone. I use my staff and go for his legs, but he manages to jump over it before it gets him down.

The song has stopped now. Either it ended or the ear buds fell out; I wasn't paying attention. This man. He's too smart to treat this like a game. This can no longer be "fun."

I swing down hard and manage to hit him on the shoulder with the staff and dislocate it, but he simply smirks and switches hands. I hate the ambidextrous. His ability to use both hands has rendered him a stronger force to be reckoned with. I'll have to take out both arms. I move to try to dislocate the other, but that is my mistake. He slashes across my chest in anticipation of my movements.

I cry out in agony and fall back. The gash in my jacket reveals that crimson has spread across my white undershirt. In his eyes, I am a fish waiting to be gutted. I have to get up and keep fighting or he'll finish me off. I begin to stand, but he dismissively kicks me back onto the ground. The sudden realization that I might die finally hits. My life practically flashes before my eyes. I think of my wife and my daughter and realize that they need me. *I'm going to die*, I think, *unless he dies first!*

In my peripheral vision, I spot my staff lying on the ground not too far away. I fumble for it, but he stomps on my leg, breaking some of the bones. I scream out in pain, but notice how openly he has exposed his leg. He's laughing, until I grab his leg and trip him. He lands on his back with a grunt and our struggle moves to the ground. I kick him back with my good leg. He slowly stands, supporting himself on a box, to get his gun which is stationed on a box not far from him. When he reaches it, he points the gun at me, but I manage to reach for my staff and whirl around to hit him as hard as I can across his jaw. I hear the sickening crack of bone as he tumbles to the ground, yelling out in pain. I slowly stand up, limping, and make my way toward him. He whirls around with the gun, holding his jaw, but I knock it out of his hand with the staff. It fires errantly as it hits the ground, making my ears ring slightly. I slam my staff onto his head, rendering him unconscious.

I check his pulse. Good, he's alive. Somehow I managed to get through this night with zero casualties. I know I won't be lucky like this again. I quickly climb up the fire escape. Up on the roof I begin to think. Tonight I could have died. I have a family at home, and they expect me to come home every night. If I keep this up, one night I inevitably won't come back. I can't do that to them. Let somebody else get in a costume and take down the scumbags. Let somebody who has nothing to lose do this. I can't be that kind of hero. I lay down my hockey mask at the scene and walk away. Not all heroes come in masks.

BREWER
The Battle of the Seven Hills

129 B.C.

Two cloaked men, one in green and the other in blue, rode into a plaza in Rome on horseback. The people there did not appear to see them, and just continued about their business. The men dismounted simultaneously, grabbed the staves that were strapped to the saddles of the horses, then walked a few steps to the fountain, which occupied the center of the plaza. They each took a handful of water from the fountain, put it to their lips, and vanished.

The two men reappeared in a circular foyer in the midst of a great crowd of cloaked men and women. The new arrivals lowered their hoods, revealing their faces like the others who hurried from place to place in the room. The man in the green cloak had long, greying hair, brown eyes, and a salt and pepper beard. His face was wizened, weathered, and thus appeared very sage. It was adorned with a rather large nose, which looked to have been broken several times. His companion looked much younger. He had long, brown hair and a full beard that was trimmed close. His green eyes showed wisdom that far exceeded his age.

The men then fought their way through the crowd that was rushing throughout the room and headed through the archways lining the circle. The men went to one of the fifteen archways that opened from the side of the circular room. Past the archway was a long, busy corridor, which the men proceeded down. At the end of this corridor, they turned left and continued down another until they reached two massive oak doors at the end of it.

The man in the green cloak raised his right hand to the crack between the two doors. The silver ring he wore on that hand touched the crack and gleamed due to the torches on either side. He whispered something and the doors opened, revealing another, slightly smaller, circular room. On its domed roof was a painting of many people fighting a great battle with hundreds of dragons. At the far end of the room was a raised platform where there was a rectangular table with five chairs, three of which were filled.

After the men had walked across the room and were about ten feet from the table, the small, portly man, seated in the middle seat and wearing a beige cloak, spoke in an affable tone, "Chancellor Gregorhoff, the Third Great Council of Light welcomes you and your apprentice back to our chambers. I trust your mission was successful."

"I am afraid it was not, Head Chancellor Jogjin. When Balregard and I arrived at the border, several Empire soldiers were there, including Hervmon himself," replied the green cloaked man, Gregorhoff.

"Hervmon himself! He is normally quite reclusive. What was he doing so near the border?" asked a woman in the second seat to the right of Jogjin.

"We too were confused, Chancellor Salima. We saw no explanation for it," said Balregard, after adjusting the left sleeve of his blue cloak.

"What happened then?" pressed the man in the first seat to the left of Jogjin.

"Very unfortunate things, Chancellor Killohan. We attempted to convince Hervmon to come back to our side," said Gregorhoff. "We entreated him to come back but he gave no indication of doing so. His reply still haunts me: 'Why would I be impelled to leave my throne as the emperor of the Second Almighty Empire of Magic to be a mere chancellor on your Council and laboriously fight a war I would never win? For if I return to you, another will take my place and carry out the goal of having only people of magic roam this world, and I will die in agony at the hands of the men that I formerly led.' Then he ordered his men to attack, and we were forced to retreat. I notice that Chancellor Magondorf is gone. Where is she?"

All of the Chancellors looked forlorn before Jogjin said, "She... she was murdered early this morning by assassins of the Empire. Hervmon is determined to have the chair that he occupied when he was a chancellor left empty at all times. We have had three chancellors murdered this month. This cannot continue."

Suddenly, warning bells started ringing, and people started shouting. The chancellors at the table bolted upright, and each grabbed their staves that were to their left, where staves were kept as the wand was held in the right, and rushed past Balregard and Gregorhoff and then out the door. The master and apprentice followed closely behind them. They proceeded down the corridor until they reached a door made of maple wood, which the group quickly filed through. When they entered, a man in a red cloak approached them.

He did the salute of the Council, his right hand in a fist over his heart, and said, "Chancellors, the War Room is at your ready."

"Thank you. Where are they attacking from?" asked Jogjin.

"Empire wizards attacked from the third and fourth hills. The thirty-fourth and twelfth legions are holding them off, but they are greatly outnumbered. The twenty-second legion is moving in as backup, but the Imperial troops severely outnumber all troops currently in Rome. We have the seventy-seventh legion and the fiftieth legions ready to move out, and several platoons also. We have sent word to the legions that are guarding Alexandria, but we doubt they can get here quick enough, even with the transport spell," replied the man.

"Get the seventy-seventh legion to go to the third hill. Salima and Killohan will lead it. Gregorhoff and Balregard will lead the fiftieth legion to the fourth hill. I want the platoons to stay here to guard Rome. Is the cloaking spell still active?" asked Jogjin.

"Yes. The civilians cannot see anyone with magical blood or the magic they produce," replied the man.

"Good. Chancellors and Balregard, get into some armor and lead your legion," ordered Jogjin.

*   *   *

Balregard and Gregorhoff rode on horseback in front of the three thousand four hundred and twelve men and women who made up the fiftieth legion. Each was armed with the weapons of sorcerers: a staff, a wand, and a ring. They were riding fast through the field that lay before the hill, and they had a mile to go before reaching it. From that distance, flashes of different colored lights produced by spells could be seen. The booms of explosive spells could be heard. The citizens of Rome, though, could see and hear none of this thanks to the cloaking spell.

When the legion reached the battle, the true numbers of the Empire could be seen. Twenty thousand were there at least. The legion rushed into the battle. Balregard and Gregorhoff dismounted and were almost instantly attacked by a man in the standard black cloak of the Empire. The man yelled out, "Kalibarus Deafimund!"

after pointing his wand at Gregorhoff. The red beam of the killing spell rushed towards the master and apprentice.

"Defenloso!" yelled out Balregard and Gregorhoff simultaneously, slamming their staves to the ground, and the shield spell formed a light blue barrier that threw the red beam into the air.

Balregard whipped his wand out from the inside of his cloak and yelled out, "Loso Juphipal!" The purple beam rushed towards the man, but he produced a shield and sent the spell flying harmlessly into the air.

Unfortunately for him, in the time that he was in combat with Balregard, Gregorhoff had slammed his staff to the ground after saying, "Solios Flimaea." The earth rippled towards the man like water then sent him flying into the air. He hit the ground with a crash and was dead. Gregorhoff and his apprentice then rushed off, deeper into the battle.

A man rushed towards Balregard whilst yelling, "Salicalisa!" His wand morphed into a great pike, with which he continued the charge. Balregard ducked and said, "Salicalisa." His wand turned into a gladius which he then drove into the gut of the man that had tripped over his ducking form. Balregard pulled the sword out and while walking away said the spell again, returning the wand to its original form.

After a few more combat situations, some closer than others, master and apprentice came across what appeared to be twenty Council soldiers combatting one Imperial soldier. Then, with a great burst of white light, the Council men flew away, dead. All was revealed when the man, cloaked in a black darker than those of most of the soldiers, turned to Gregorhoff and Balregard. His long, dark hair, his well-trimmed black goatee, and his dark eyes showed them that it was the Emperor himself. The master and apprentice were astonished that the Emperor was attacking Rome. They quickly overcame this surprise, as this was the battle for the capital of the Council, so where else would the Emperor be? Two Imperial soldiers rushed to engage the master and apprentice, but the Emperor waved them off.

"They are mine," he said in a cool and calm voice.

"Balregard, get behind me," said Gregorhoff quietly.

"So we meet again Chancellor Gregoroff the Green. And your apprentice Balregard the Blue," said the Emperor.

"I was suspecting you would be here after this morning, Chancellor Hervmon the Black," replied Gregorhoff.

"That is Emperor Hervmon to you," he said.

"I call you Chancellor because we served together as them, and you betrayed them," said Gregorhoff.

"So be it," said Hervmon, raising his wand, "Kalibarus Deafimund!" Gregorhoff flicked his wand and blocked it with ease then sent the killing spell at Hervmon who also blocked it.

"Salicalisa!" yelled Hervmon. His wand morphed into a battle-ax and he charged. Gregorhoff performed the same spell, his wand changing into a spatha, and caught the blow that would have chopped off his right leg.

Gregorhoff pushed Hervmon back, and sent a green beam from his ring. Hervmon blocked it with his ring, then, having morphed the ax back to a wand, again sent the killing spell at Gregorhoff. It was blocked, and countered with a purple beam. So it continued for an hour, switching from melee to ring to stave to wand constantly until red sparks flew into the sky over Rome, the sign that the Council chambers had been captured.

The Empire had forced its way through on the third hill and had taken Rome. Wizards and Witches of the Council started vanishing into a poof of smoke as they teleported away. Rome had fallen. When Gregorhoff saw the sparks, he ran to where Balregard was battling, dodged a spell sent by Hervmon, and grabbed his shoulder.

Gregorhoff yelled out, "Dismolevar!" The two vanished into smoke, then reappeared somewhere else: Alexandria.

"Rome fell," said Gregorhoff "The capital of both the lands of the Third Great Council of Light and the Roman Empire are now in the hands of the Hervmon."

"Will we ever return?" asked Balregard, after seeing the look of dread in his master's eyes.

"Return. Yes, but it will be a long time from now. When we do return though, Hervmon better be ready, for we will not only be stronger and more powerful than ever, but we will also be there with the one tool that he has not anticipated... vengeance."

9
BROOME
The Mystery
of the Mysterious Clicks

Zdeno was casually walking home from school on August 11, 2137. He was thinking about how utterly horrible his favorite hockey team, the Boston Mooins, had played the season before and what they needed to fix to be competent next season. They were the elite team of the league and had played well in the normal season, but they blew it in the playoffs. They had the third round playoff spot in their hands. All they needed to do was keep up their defenses and score one goal, but his favorite player, Marchand VII, missed four open shots in a row and the California Golden Seals, the team they were playing, scored. They left the ice defeated. All of a sudden, the distinct clicking of an electronic keyboard, the kind of sound his iPhone made when he typed on it, whispered to him. It seemed to summon Zdeno. He went still for a moment but then he resumed his walk. He looked around to see if other people could hear the clicks too, but no one else seemed to be reacting. Zdeno was very confused and was afraid to follow the sound, but when he heard it for a second time, he felt a strange feeling; he felt like he needed to retrieve whatever was producing it.

Zdeno followed the repetitive clicks, making sure not to overlook any place where it could possibly be. It summoned him like some sort of witchcraft. It frightened him, but it brought him in at the same time. He looked inside trash cans, on the ground, and in every box he could find, but there was no trace of the object that was clicking. "Ugh!" groaned Zdeno, becoming frustrated with the three hour hunt. Finally, he deduced that the sounds were getting louder and softer each direction that he moved. He assumed that the clicking would be loudest where the origin of the sound was.

Across streets, around town, and through the whole city of Boston, Zdeno listened for the clicking. He followed it until he was at a construction site. There, the clicking was so loud that he could hardly hear anything else. He was exhausted by the four hour search, exhilarated by the sheer mystery of the clicking, and worried that his mother would be mad at him for being so late home from school.

He tracked the clicking down and found that it was coming from inside a wall of dirt in the soon-to-be foundation of the Patrice Bergeron Memorial museum. As he dug into the wall using his hands, he contemplated what would be behind the layer of sediment. After a few minutes of digging, an old, dingy box was revealed. As soon as it was in sight, the clicking stopped. He took it out and stared in wonder of what could possibly be inside.

Zdeno ran back home, and the sun had set by the time he was back at his house. He hid the box from his infuriated, yelling, and red faced mother and ran upstairs to his room. "This box must be wicked old!" exclaimed Zdeno. He opened it up and examined the contents. There was nothing in there except for some sort of box. He felt the few buttons on the smaller box and thought it was a cell phone. He didn't recognize the model, so he used his Google photo-searching app and Google told him that it was an iPhone 5! Since it was his bedtime and his mother was already mad at him, Zdeno decided to hide the box beneath a pile of clothes in his closet and show it to his friend Tukka the next day.

The next day after school, Zdeno was grounded for staying out so late. He wasn't allowed to use anything electronic, leave the house, or have any friends over. However, since his mom was gone, he invited Tukka over anyways. Zdeno had told him about the find at school that day, and they were both excited. "Do you think it could've been made before the iPhone 60th!?" asked Tukka with excitement in his voice and adventure in his eye.

"Google said it's an iPhone 5!" replied Zdeno. "Those models are even older than my parents!" They examined it more and, using the internet, reassured themselves that it indeed was an iPhone model five. "Wow" was all Zdeno could think to say.

"This must be the biggest fossil find of the year!" replied Tukka. Both boys were dumbfounded by how old the phone was. Since it worked similarly to their current model iPhone, Zdeno turned it on and unlocked it. He and Tukka stared in awe at the low quality screen with ancient icons for the applications. "It's so heavy, short, and wide!" exclaimed Tukka. He pulled out his iPhone 83 and it was 2 inches longer, a quarter inch thinner, and a half pound lighter!

Zdeno and Tukka searched all the applications to see what it was like and started to fiddle with the settings and preferences. All of a sudden, a whirlwind rose and the papers in the room were swept off of the tables and desks in the bedroom. They both shook in fear. Then a man started to materialize out of the cell phone. Soon enough, there was a man standing in the room with them.

The boys were terrified. "Who are you?" Zdeno asked. They were both shaking with fear as he looked at them.

"I am Steve Jobs," the man replied. "I am the inventor of the iPhone and I have been buried alive inside this iPhone for decades."

"But you died a hundred years ago!" trembled Tukka as his hands shook in fear.

"I can understand why you would think this. I never actually died, I was consumed by that iPhone. I was studying the iPhone for faults to improve it for my next model, when I suddenly was sucked in," replied Jobs sadly.

"My mother has warned me about that!" Zdeno replied.

"Me too!" shouted Tukka. "But I never thought that she was serious."

"Yes, I am afraid that it is very serious. Spending too much time on your iPhone really will suck you into it, and the consequences are terrible. I wasted my life away with it. I have survived decades of incredibly lagging internet, updates that mean nothing and are hardly compatible with the phone, and incredibly annoying and addictive arcade games!"

"That sounds terrible!" replied Tukka.

"It sounds like Apple to me," smirked Zdeno.

k
BROWN
Hero

"Come on! Let's go in here!" Ally shouted while pulling Hailey and Darcy into a clothing store.

"Ugh, we've been shopping for a million years!" Hailey exaggerated.

Ally and Darcy just rolled their eyes as they entered the store. The girls all went in separate directions looking at all of the different clothing and accessories in the store. Darcy picked out some shirts and other items and headed to the fitting room to try them on.

The lady running the fitting rooms had an austere dress on that didn't particularly match the vibrant and preppy theme of the store. Her hair was in a bun on the top of her head, and she had an expression on her face that made her look like she was the unhappiest person to ever live. Darcy hesitantly asked for a fitting room, and the lady reluctantly opened up a door for her. Darcy entered and shut the door behind her. In the middle of trying on clothes, a loud boom reverberated throughout the mall. Darcy could hear the faint screams from across the mall in the fitting room. The screams were cut off by the screeching of the fire alarms.

Still clad in the store's clothes, Darcy hastily slipped back into her original clothes and hurried out of the dressing room and back into the store. The lady working in the fitting rooms along with Darcy's friends and the other shoppers that had been in the store were now gone. Darcy started walking towards the door, but it was suddenly engulfed in flames. The flames gave off thick smoke that pervaded the store, making it hard to breathe. Darcy knew that she needed to get out before the flames came further into the store. She spotted an air vent on the wall across from her. She crawled over to it and endeavored to get the bolts out of the wall, but they wouldn't budge. Now despondent, the thought that she would be stuck here haunted her. All she could do was scream for help in the hope that someone could hear her.

"Help! Help! Help!" Darcy repeated over and over again.

It had now been twenty minutes and smoke covered the whole store. Darcy could no longer yell. The only sounds she could make were those of her coughs. The flames had made their way further into the store, and Darcy was losing strength. Darcy felt like she would pass out any minute, and she could no longer stand. She saw a figure approach the flaming doorway. As the figure moved closer, Darcy realized that it was a fireman. Once right in front of the flames, the anonymous man briskly walked through them, not being burned due to the fireproof suit he was wearing. Darcy called out again, so the fireman could hear her because the smoke was too thick to see through clearly. He walked over to Darcy and told her that his name was John, and he was going to help her get out. John bent down, picked up Darcy, and carried her back through the flames, holding her up so she wouldn't get burned.

They had almost made it to the door when the ceiling gave in to the turbulent flames on the floor above and came crashing down towards Darcy and John. Before it could land on both of them, John threw Darcy in the direction of the door, and she hit the ground with a thud. When Darcy looked up, all she could see was the gruesome look on John's face, and he screamed out in excruciating pain as the ceiling covered him. While one fireman carried her away and the other went to check on John, she watched as he faded away. She was greeted by her friends outside of the mall and put in an ambulance. That was the last time she ever saw John. As the ambulance drove away from the mall, Darcy knew that shopping wouldn't ever be the same again.

brooke
BRYANT
Princeton & the Twins

Once upon a time in a faraway land, there was an evil teenage boy named Princeton. He and his younger, affable step brothers, Tim and Jim, lived with his step dad, Robby. Princeton has always been jealous of the twins because of how much more popular they were than him. So, one morning in late spring, Tim and Jim were talking before school, as they always did. But that day in particular they were talking about Lacey, Jim's crush and her Sweet 16 Party. And Princeton, having nothing better to do, decided to eavesdrop on their conversation. Hearing the news that Jim liked Lacey made him wince. Princeton was disgusted at the idea of Jim and Lacey together. Especially when he had liked her since Kindergarten, but she never gave him the time of day. Princeton was appalled and began to meditate on a plan to ruin any chance Jim had with her. He was not going to let Jim take the only girl he had ever liked.

As Princeton and his brothers got on the bus for school, Princeton kept thinking of how he was going to thank Lacey for the invitation to her Sweet 16 Party. He was frantic because she was giving them out today, and he wanted to be ready. When they got to Lacey's stop, he began to grow excited. Lacey got on the bus and waved to him and kept walking down the aisle like she did every day. At first he thought she might be waiting to pass them out at school, but when she stood in the middle of the aisle and handed Tim and Jim an invitation, he was furious. He grew angrier and angrier throughout first and second block. Then, when he went to his locker at the end of the school day, an invitation was taped to the front of it.

Filled with exhilaration, after school Princeton drove to the mall to buy a suit and tie for Lacey's party, the following night. While shopping, he picked a navy blue suit and tie because it was austere, and he hated being flashy. Little did he know that his brothers were going shopping for the party too. But they went home, did their homework, and then drove to the mall. By that time, Princeton was already back at home and since he rarely paid attention to them, he didn't even notice they were gone. That night at dinner, Princeton excused himself from the table because he had to use the restroom. On his way back, he saw two identical navy blue suits and ties in the twins' room. The twins had the exact same suit and tie as Princeton. After seeing this, he was furious and reacted quickly: he ran into their room and ripped the suits and ties to pieces. He made sure not to overlook any pieces of fabric. In order for him not to get caught, it was vital that he went back to dinner before anyone was done. Then they would think the dog, Elvis, did it. Later that night, when Tim and Jim found all their stuff ruined, they were devastated and knew that Princeton had something to do with it. But they didn't bother telling Robby because they didn't want to seem like tattletales. They were mostly upset because of the expenditure. The twins had spent all their allowances combined on their outfits for the party. Not to mention if they wore their suits and ties to the party now, they would be utterly see through.

The next day was the day of the party, which for Princeton was exciting, but for the twins not so much. When they all got home from school, Princeton began to get ready for the party, while the twins just mopped around and watched TV. About thirty minutes went by when Robby left to go to the store and Princeton headed out for the party. Just when Tim and Jim were about to go to sleep they a heard a weird knock on the window. Very casually they went over to the window to see what it was. To their surprise it was Robby in a limo with two suits and ties. Tim and Jim were overjoyed and asked sarcastically "Are you our fairy god father?" They all laughed. On the way to the party, they changed, and Robby made them promise to be home by twelve. When they finally arrived at the party they were a little hesitant at first of what Princeton might do, but then they decided to make a gambit and go for it. As soon as Princeton found out the twins were there, he started his mischief to keep Jim away from Lacey. He didn't think the twins would show up, but to insure that he didn't have a lapse of judgement he was prepared anyway. He got skunk spray from a store in the mall, downloaded a burping app on his phone, and got laughing liquid. First he hid under the drink table which was where Lacey and Jim were talking, and sprayed skunk spray all around them until the smell festered. Next, he hid behind the coat rack which was where they moved after the smell overpowered the drink table. Then, while Jim was talking to Lacey, Princeton used his burping app to make it look like Jim had started burping uncontrollably in the middle of his sentence. At first they were both still for a few moments then Lacey excused herself to go to the restroom (really just as an excuse to get out of the conversation).

After a while, Lacey began to notice that every time something bad happened, Princeton was around, so she started to watch him closely. Then she finally caught him: he was spiking Jim's drink with laughing liquid. After that, she knew it was the last straw so she yelled at him, and kicked him out of the party. Then she went back over to the drink table where Jim was waiting for her. He thanked her and kissed her on the cheek intimately. And they lived happily ever after, well except for Princeton. Robby finally got tired of all his mischief and sent him to military school.

anna
BURKE
The Disgruntled Elf

As I walked through The North Pole Courtyard, I saw Santa Claus laboriously grooming his reindeer. He was clad in his ugly red suit and out of style matching hat. While I continued to judge his poor outfit choice, I heard a loud thump and walked over to retrieve the reins that Dasher had squirmed out of. I gingerly fed Dasher a rather large carrot to keep him occupied while I modified his reins and Ol' Saint Nick inspected Vixen's hooves. I really liked the reindeer; however, I couldn't say that I felt the same way about Santa. There was something about him that was almost *too* jolly. "Well, thank you very much Tinsel! These bulls have been extremely sensitive lately. Ho! Ho! Ho!"

"Mmm hmm," I said coolly.

"Tinsel, we need more elves like you. You're always helping out and never complaining. You certainly have the Christmas spirit! Now run along, you have some toys to make!"

Well, that's me: Tinsel the tiny tinker elf! I'm one of thousands in the Elf Society who spend 364 days a year making toy cars and stuffed unicorns for some little spoiled brat to wake up to on Christmas morning. Then, the clueless child thanks Santa and frames the picture they took with him at the mall. But why? It's not like Santa made any of the toys! The only thing that old fatty did was ride in his sleigh for one night, being pulled along by his poor reindeer.

Now, you might be wondering, "Tinsel, what do Santa's selfless elves get in return for being his personal minions all throughout the interminable days spent toiling in the factory?" The answer is: a half-pound of candy a day, and a tiny, utterly austere shack to live in. The candy is enough to keep us going on a constant sugar-high, but it rots our poor teeth and makes us chubby. The shacks he makes us live in are almost smaller than him! We are forced to have the same Christmas themed sheets and hideous furniture. The shacks are plain, boring, and repulsively decorated. Also, Kris Kringle is too cheap to pay for our insurance! That means no dental plan and no coverage for the damage an elf might inflict on his home during an intense sugar rush. The more that I thought about it, the more I realized just how unfair Santa had been treating us all these years!

As I squeezed through the entrance to my shack, a brilliant idea came to me. If I revealed to the other elves how bad of a boss Santa was, maybe they would agree with me, and we could all change Santa into the ideal head of The North Pole. If it worked, he would give us the insurance we needed and a candy pay-raise! But first, I'd have to convince the other elves. I thought for a long time before coming up with the perfect plan. I would summon everyone to an emergency Elf Society meeting, and then I would tell them my plan for boosting our benefits.

I printed out flyers advertising the meeting that would take place in exactly twenty-four hours. After that, I hurried out into the courtyard and taped them on the red and green benches, candy cane striped lampposts, and the huge sleigh that was parked in front of the toy factory. The good thing was that news travelled fast in the Elf Society. Just last week, a rumor that I was being named Santa's favorite elf spread across the entire factory in less than ten minutes! Unfortunately, it wasn't true. Anyway, within a few hours, every single elf would know about the meeting I was calling for. When I got home, I got in my tiny bed that fit perfectly in my tiny room inside my depressingly tiny shack. As I pulled the ugly Christmas themed sheets up to my pointy ears, I realized how excited I was about my plan, and I couldn't wait to see how the next day would turn out!

"Welcome, fellow elves! I'm glad that everybody showed up. This meeting is very important! It's the first step we're taking towards our news lives," I said. With this, everybody shared confused looks with each other. "Let me explain," I continued. "Santa is a cheapskate. We cannot overlook the unfair treatment any longer. We deserve better! I have come up with a plan to ensure that we get exactly what we want: a candy pay raise, along with home and health insurance. Also, our shacks need some serious upgrades! I propose that we get Santa to remodel our humble neighborhoods! We will demand our salary be raised from half a pound to a full pound of delicious sweets! All we have to do is bombard his nice mansion with snowballs, and maybe we'll even wrap his trees. It'll be fun! We can make it so that he'll have to agree to our terms. He leaves us no option."

"I agree with Tinsel!" shouted one elf.

"Me, too!" called another.

Soon, all the elves agreed and couldn't wait to spring into action. We would all meet again at midnight, pelt Santa's house with snowballs, and wrap his trees with cheerful Christmas wrapping paper. All that I had to do until then was sneak into the wrapping department, which had been closed for two weeks due to a fire that had been started by an elf on a sugar rush, and grab as many rolls of colorful paper as possible. I waited until Santa and all the other elves had left, and then I snuck into the factory. As I walked calmly through the singed doors, I saw a gleam of reflective "Feliz Navidad" paper that had survived the fire. I grabbed the roll, along with a few others that read, "Happy Birthday Jesus" and "Lighten Up. It's Christmas!" I made a clean exit and rushed to meet the other elves in the courtyard. It was ten till midnight.

We arrived at Santa's elaborate mansion at 12:15 AM. The mansion was peaceful, and all the lights were off. I found it interesting that his house was bigger than the entire elf neighborhood! He had elaborate fountains, Christmas sculptures, and dozens of guest rooms for when his friends, such as the Easter Bunny and Mother Nature, came to visit.

"It's time for your wakeup call, Mr. Claus," I laughed with the other elves. As I passed out the wrapping paper, the other elves prepared the snowballs. We all took our positions, aimed, and fired. With perfect precision, we pelted his windows and door. We cheered whenever a snowball disappeared down his chimney. Soon, his lights were on, and we could heard him waddling down the stairs. Santa opened his front door, and before he could get a word out, he was soaked in freezing cold snow and ice. Shivering, he looked up at his trees now reading "Feliz Navidad" and "Happy Birthday Jesus" and then over at his bushes that were completely covered in "Lighten Up. It's Christmas!"

He looked terrified for a brief moment, before bursting out in his typical, "Ho! Ho! Ho!"

"Good morning, Father Christmas," I said sarcastically.

"Good morning, Tinsel. I love what you've done with the place," he said a little *too* cheerfully.

"Mr. Claus, we're here because you have been treating us unfairly! We deserve a raise. As of now, half a pound of candy barely lasts us the day; however, a full pound would be much more appropriate, don't you think?"

"Well, considering I'm always in the giving mood and your requests don't sound unreasonable, I'm sure that can be arranged," Santa proclaimed.

"Good! And with all that extra sugar, insurance will be vital!"

"Insurance for what, Tinsel?" He seemed relaxed, like he had been expecting these complaints.

"Well, you know how destructive some elves tend to be when they overdose on sugar. Might I remind you of the wrapping department incident? So, we want home insurance to protect what's ours! Also, we need bigger shacks. These living arrangements just aren't cutting it. We also need health insurance, Mr. Kringle. All the sugar is bad for our teeth, and it doesn't agree with everyone's stomach," I informed him.

"Okay, Tinsel. I agree to your terms. Thank you for your honesty and free house decorating! I told you that you had the Christmas spirit!"

"Thank you, Santa," I said as we all cheered and encompassed Santa in a big group hug.

"So, everybody," Santa began as the elves quieted down, "I think that this calls for a celebration! How about tomorrow, you can all help me test fly the reindeer? Christmas is right around the corner, and I need to be sure that they can all still fly and follow directions. Tinsel is great with the reindeer, so he can be the leader tomorrow," Santa proclaimed.

The next day, Santa followed through and put me in charge of the reindeer. I could tell the animals were happy to see me, and so were the other elves! Everybody was in a good mood. All day long, I got to help my friends test-fly the reindeer, and as I watched Dancer fly high above the toy factory, I realized that life at the North Pole was pretty great!

m
COLLINS

I woke up feeling confident about what seemed like the hundredth gypsy essay. Our third block was unfortunately writing yet another four paragraph essay on why Holmes dressed as a gypsy in the novel *The Beekeeper's Apprentice* written by Laurie King. I get up feeling pretty amazing about this one due to my growth in writing essays throughout the year in Mr. Wilson's class.

I arrive at the entrance of Mr. Wilson's room. I take my seat quietly and wait to receive the test we get every Wednesday. As Mr. Wilson enters the room, he tells everyone to pull out the gypsy essay. I obediently pull the sheet of paper out of my folder from underneath my desk. I scan over the paper one last time, trying not to overlook any mistakes. This paper was not going to be just competent. Our class had to rewrite this essay over many times due to lack of quality, so we wanted this to be the last gypsy essay, once and for all. Therefore, it was vital that it be in tip top shape. Finally out of realization that mostly everyone else had passed their papers in, I reluctantly handed in mine.

As Mr. Wilson returned to his desk, I started on my test. The test was over italics, underlining, and quotations. It was excruciating! He began grading the essays while I anticipated my good grade. I looked back and counted down to my paper due to the stack being in alphabetical order. I noticed how he graded everyone else's paper: a slash every here and there. As he arrived at my essay, I see the green pen make more slashes throughout my writing than normal. I then hear "Collins." I cast my attention to the back of the room toward Mr. Wilson once again. Usually when someone is called back to his desk, it is not a very good thing. I hesitantly rise out of my chair and head toward the back of the room.

As I approach, I speculate something is wrong after seeing Mr. Wilson's bleak expression. He, all of a sudden, points his finger toward my assignment. He begins to ask me what is wrong with the sentence that obtained a big green slash through it. I sit, searching for the mistake that he was looking for. I looked at the citation, commas, and finally the quotations. After finding the error, I sat appalled at what I had forgotten to include. I stood in a state of bewilderment as I quickly looked around the room due to my shock at the situation. I begin telling him that I dropped a quote in my paragraph without my own words around it.

He agrees and explains to me that I will be receiving a 1/55, which is a one point eight in the gradebook. I never expected that I would be one of the people making this massive mistake. This obviously dropped my overall grade in English quite a bit. I tried, as discreetly as possible, to return to my seat. I felt like the walls were closing in on me. The moment kept recurring in my brain, haunting me. Though I did not shed a tear in that room, I couldn't help myself when I got home. At first I thought the idea of giving me a one was despicable, but it soon became evident to me that you can learn from your mistakes. And we all know I never made that mistake again. NEVER drop a quote! It doesn't look very good in the gradebook, and it will go poorly for you.

andrew
CROCKETT
Smells like Trouble

Yesterday, I went to bed the same way as I always do; in my favorite shirt, in my bed, in my apartment. However, when I woke up this morning, something was different. I woke up in nice clothes, in a nicer bed, and with an ID and passport sitting right by the bed for me to see. It wasn't me or my name, and worst of all, I had a different face, I still looked like me just younger

Now I was supposedly John Smith, and I lived in a new house, luckily in the same city. Also, instead of being 36, I am supposedly 24. As I looked around this new house, I found pictures of me from college. The decorations made it feel like I was still there. I found a note in the kitchen that said to go to 1550 Jefferson Street where I will see a man in a suit who will give me further instructions. I didn't know what to expect.

1550 Jefferson Street was 15 miles away, and I wasn't going to walk. My new wallet didn't have a metro pass, so I couldn't take a subway. In this new identity I don't have a car, so I had to take a taxi. When I flagged one down and told him the address he said, "Oh no, taxis don't go back there. Its too dangerous." I asked him why it was so dangerous and he said, "That is *Wolf Pack*, a gang known for violence and big wolf tattoos, territory, and he would be mugged in a heartbeat." That did not make the situation any better.

I eventually got on Uber, an app that lets you hire someone to drive you wherever, and found someone who would give me a ride. There was only one person who said they were going back there. The driver had a giant wolf tattoo with a crown on his right shoulder, which means that he is probably the leader of Wolf Pack. That's when I knew I was going to a bad place.

When I got there, I found the only guy wearing anything remotely nice and asked him what was going on. He said, "Walk straight down 3rd avenue until the end, but stay as close to the buildings as you can." I said ok, but why, but he just kept repeating, "Walk straight down 3rd avenue until the end, but stay as close to the buildings as you can."

I knew that area and knew it was better than where I was, but it was not that much better. Taxis would go to 3rd avenue, so I got a taxi and went there. I swear this taxi driver was on something. He swerved back and forth between cars in a very erratic way. I was tremulous. When he finally became still after my entreaties, I gave him a very long tirade about safe driving. That's when police encompassed the car, pulled me out, arrested that guy for an unknown reason. Luckily, he had already gotten me to where I needed to go.

I walked down the road on the side closest to the buildings as I had been told. I made a few stops at some stores on this row and shopped. When I got about 2/3 of the way down the strip, everything changed. Someone jumped out from an alley, and I was grabbed and dragged to a dark van just on the other side. I endeavored to escape, but failed, and I had to succumb to the kidnapper. In the van, I did everything Liam Neeson would have done: I remembered key things I heard and felt, and I took off the blindfold that was over my eyes. We went up a big hill and then turned left, and I could hear trains. I quickly realized we were in the remote manufacturing district. We made an abrupt stop, and I could hear the guys get out of the front seat and come my way. They grabbed me and dragged me out of the van, but right before the kidnapper covered my eyes again, I saw where I was.

They had taken me to the old meat processing plant. I knew this building like the back of my hand because my dad used to work here, and I went to work with him a lot. They walked me inside and took me to the main meat room. All of the sudden through the translucent cloth on my eyes, I was blinded by a very bright gleam light. That's when I heard a brusque voice say, "What do you smell?"

I had totally forgotten to smell the place because I was so scared. For an old meat processing plant, it smelled really good, so I told him, and he took the blindfold off. I saw rotten meat and bugs and a lot of signs that said Freshie air freshener on them. Instead of huge kidnappers, I saw a bunch of affable people with cameras. I was bewildered. They said that I was in a Freshie commercial, which is a common air freshener brand.

I asked them why they changed my look, name, and house, and they responded, "Your name is weird, you are ugly, and we wanted you to feel like you were still in college." They showed me the concise commercial and gave me my old life back. My ID and passport, my house, and my metro card. It was almost back to normal except for one thing: my face was still different. But it was a good different because I looked younger. It was all starting to make sense. That is when I woke up.

† DENTON

I remember that horrid day of the English test. I had no affection towards it. It all started about 2 weeks ago, as a casual day. I got out of bed, got dressed, ate breakfast, brushed my teeth, and boarded the bus to school. There wasn't any sun though because it had been raining all morning. I knew that the test was awaiting me, but sadly, I didn't study. I started out okay, walking into the school like normal. I went to the gym and sat down on the bleachers, waiting for the bell to ring. I was talking to my buddies to pass the interminable time. We were talking about random subjects like the latest things happening around the school and recent assignments such as essays, vocab, and worksheets.

Suddenly, the bell rang. I started heading to my English class. When I got there, I prepared myself for the test by looking over my very few notes. Once class started, we did the moment of silence and "Pledge of Allegiance." Then, we took the test. I was pretty sure I failed it because I didn't study at all. The day after the test was the real problem, even though I was afraid of what I would get. Apparently, I got mere *D*. I would just conceal that grade from my parents. I was more concerned with what other people got because there were other grades like mine. Everyone had a low grade!

Then, I heard Mr. Wilson laughing over the reaction of the class, which enraged the students, and they went mad! They flipped over desks, and they trashed the classroom with graded papers. It looked like a tornado went through the classroom. Luckily, all of the desks were intact. Some students were crying, while others were either laughing or destroying the classroom. Some students entreated Mr. Wilson to let them retake the test. Each person had their own, distinct way of showing how they felt towards Mr. Wilson. I wasn't really angry because the grade I got was better than I thought it would be. I thought that I was the most behaved person there at the time because I wasn't doing anything wrong.

Later, while the classroom was calming down, Mr. Wilson was listening to music, and when everyone was done trashing the room, he explained that he gave us the bad grades out of spite, and because it was April Fool's Day! He was quite angry over the fact that the entire classroom was demolished. He said that he would let us retake the test! He did receive an abundance of e-mails from parents as a result. He apologized to the parents and explained that it was a joke. We also had to restore Mr. Wilsons classroom back to normal, and most students got in trouble. I was just happy that I would actually get a chance to study this time.

alexias
EHIEMUA
The Campfire

"Let's go outside and have a campfire!" Mary-Kate said as she put on her favorite pair of fuzzy pink slippers. She had her best friends, Kelly and Camille, over for their monthly sleepover. She had been begging her mom to let her have a campfire for the longest time. However, her mom reasoned she was too irresponsible; her room was always messy, and she never did her homework. Since then, Mary-Kate had been doing her chores, and helping her parents around the house. They finally let her have a campfire, but what Mary-Kate didn't know was that this campfire had been planned for over a month.

"Can I come, too?" Will, Mary-Kate's little brother, fervently begged.

"No!" Mary-Kate, Camille, and Kelly rebuffed.

"I'm going to get you back for this!" Will called back, as he angrily stomped up the stairs.

The girls rolled their eyes, put on their slippers, and rushed out to the patio.

"I just love campfires!" exclaimed Camille.

"Do we have to stay out here? You guys know I hate bugs," Kelly complained.

"Come on, Kelly. I promise you'll relish this moment forever!" Camille said.

"Fine. But as soon as a bug comes near me, I'm leaving," said Kelly.

When the girls went outside, there were sleeping bags, a small fire, marshmallows, graham crackers, and chocolate. "I have to admit, this is pretty cool. And I haven't seen any bugs yet," said Kelly. All of the girls laughed as they walked over to the crackling fire. They were all having a blast; they told scary ghost stories and ate s'mores. Before they knew it, it was 1:30 am! They needed to get ready for bed because they had school tomorrow.

"Best campfire ever," Mary-Kate said.

A few hours later, the girls were awoken by a loud SNAP!

"What was that?" Camille asked, her heart beating out of her chest.

"I'm sure it was nothing," Mary-Kate said, trying to keep everyone calm. But it came again, SNAP! This one sounded closer.

"Uh, maybe we should go inside," Kelly frantically suggested.

"No!" Mary-Kate profoundly exclaimed, "How about we find out what it is?" Mary-Kate grabbed the flashlight by her bag and started heading towards the woods. "Guys, I found something!" Mary-Kate dragged the mysterious box behind her. "This thing weighs two tons," she complained. She opened it and found a strange note:

> Roses are red, violets are blue
> You may not know me but I know you
> Don't tell anyone or you will find out
> What happens when a girl won't shut her mouth

The girls looked at the papers that followed. There were instructions they had to do for each day of the week. They read the instructions for Monday through Friday and were terrified.

"I don't think we should do the instructions for Friday," Mary-Kate said in tremulous a voice.

"Yeah, I would never hurt you guys like that," added Kelly.

"Let's just worry about it when it comes. It's already late, and we have to get to school tomorrow," said Camille, ending the conversation. The girls went to sleep, knowing what they had coming up the following week. Monday, they had to wear the tackiest outfits they could find to school. Mary-Kate wore her hair in pigtails and had on her baby doll costume from Halloween; Kelly and Camille wore their matching red and blue Thing 1 and Thing 2 costumes from two years ago that barely fit. Everyone made fun of them for the whole day. Even the teachers laughed a little.

Tuesday, they were all forced to stay out late in a coffee shop and miss curfew. When their parents asked why they missed curfew, they had to come up with a lie. No matter how bad they wanted to tell the truth. They were all grounded for two weeks.

Wednesday, they all skipped school and had to host a party while their parents were at work. There were over 200 people, and the house was a mess when Mary-Kate's parents got home. They were all grounded for another two weeks, and they were suspended from school for a week.

Thursday, they each had to take one significant item that belonged to one of their family members. Mary-Kate took her dad's 30 carat gold watch, Camille took her mom's diamond earrings, and Kelly took her sister's favorite pearl necklace. Friday, they had to sell those materials, and were told to blame one another for doing so.

"There's no way I'm doing this!" Mary-Kate said.

"What else are we going to do?" asked Camille, "We can't tell them the truth."

"That's our only other option," said Kelly.

They decided to tell their parents everything. No matter how much it hurt them. After they gathered their family members, the girls all sat down and took a deep breath.

"Listen, we haven't been completely honest with you guys this past week," Mary-Kate started.

"And that's why we were acting crazy," Kelly said.

"We couldn't have told you guys the truth or else something really bad would've happened to all of us," said Camille.

They told their parents everything, from start to finish. After they finished, their parents stood there with grimaces on their faces. Everyone was silent.

"We need to go to the police right now," Mary-Kate's father said, raging with anger.

"Um, maybe we shouldn't go." Will said, nervously. "It's not that serious, and no one has gotten hurt."

"This isn't just some game, Will. We don't know who this person is, or how they know us," said Kelly.

"I'm the mysterious person behind the chest," he finally admitted, "I told you I'd get you back for not letting me come to the campfire with you guys."

"You're dead meat," said Mary-Kate as she chased him up the stairs.

dylan
ERWIN
Boats

The year was 1912, and I was a part of a mission to go to space. On the way back to Earth, my capsule hit something while it was falling. BANG! it sounded like it was something metal, so I knew something was wrong. I opened the capsule door, leaving it slightly ajar. I knew it was a boat because it was round and fat like a pig but yet like a bird because it was flying. That's how I realized I was on an airboat. I contemplated what to do because I didn't want to fall off and land in front of a bus. I'm sure if I did fall I would probably only get a small abrasion. I know that because it's happened to my friend before.

I tried to climb to a window, but before I could, a strong gust of wind blew me off, and I started to fall. I landed on a pile of mattresses on a different type of boat. I thought the deck was talking to me. Then I realized decks can't talk, so I knew it couldn't be that. It was an affable man who was asking me what happened with a strange look on his face. He ran quickly to tell the doctor on the ship, so they could make sure I was ok. It was a boat. A boat-boat. I knew that because I saw water. Last time I checked, objects that are like giant fat children can't hold people nor can they float so I knew it was a ship. I loved it because it was such a nice elegant ship. I decided to live on it.

There I was, on the beautiful *Titanic* slashing through the waves of an ocean. I knew I was on it because I had evidence. That was the fact that I asked the weird man who saw me on the mattresses. The English language also chose to italicize other boats as well just not quite the ones that sink and cause a catastrophe in the middle of ice waters. All boats are loud when going through the noisy ocean, and they are annoying. You may be thinking that they are like big fat babies but the difference is babies don't float. I know you were fooled, but that's ok because you didn't know if floaties were involved. I couldn't believe I was there. I was bewildered so I had traced my day back to see how I had gotten there.

There are also loud and round airplanes which of course are called airboats. Calling them airboats may seem kind of obscure, but it's not one bit. Airboats are like a fat birds with navigation and landing gear. Except last time I checked, riding a bird thousands of feet up may or may not result in death. Also when a bird goes off course, there aren't tiny people in its brain freaking out when they can't fix it. They both, however, land in water except when the bird does, it gets eaten by giant alligators. Fortunately, airboats aren't eaten by alligators very often. The only time it has happened is when an airboat called *US Airlines flight 1549* crashed into the Hudson river and a dragon-sized alligator came out of the water and swallowed the plane whole. Birds also aren't as loud. To compare them, you have to imagine a bird singing in the sky for no reason and as loud as a rocket ship. When I had landed on an airboat I went to the window and sardonically grinned to freak out the passengers.

A spaceboat is a rocket ship. It has a round shape and is pointed like a triangle at the top. They are my favorite because the ships go high in the sky. So high that it's a million times higher than a fat bird flying in the sky. They are the loudest of all the boats. People often have trouble telling if it's a spaceboat or Khrushchev's mixtape. Sending his mixtape is good advertising so people never know the difference and depending on how good it is, it could be electrifying. It makes the statement that his mixtape will reach the moon before you. More often than not, it's just a spaceboat because he only releases his mixtape when he bangs his shoe or when he has to bury people. Many people still abhor spaceboats after what happened in 1986, also known as the year the Challenger blew up.

Whether they are fat babies, birds, or mixtapes, people love watching them as they are as beautiful as the original boats they are. Although they are very similar, there are slight differences between them which makes it hard to precisely know which one is which. So basically boats are as loud and annoying as giant versions of living things such as babies and birds, and sometimes a nice mixtape every once in a while. The mixtapes aren't usually accessible and are only competent when they are back on earth. NASA usually only sends up spaceboats. I don't think I need to elaborate any more for you to understand what the boats are like. You may wonder why these are different boats and why they are italicized. The reason is because of old dead white guys. That's it, there are no other reasons behind it.

g
GALLON

The day had finally come. Travis was graduating from Vanderbilt University, and he was excited about graduating. It had been a long four years studying psychology. Travis was glad that he was finally done with school. After receiving his diploma, he met with his ecstatic parents. "We are so proud of you, son. Because of your tremendous accomplishments, we are excited to tell you that we are sending you on a trip to England, all expenses paid. We thought that once you were there, you could meet up with your friends from middle school who moved: Jimmy and Brandon," his mother explained to him. Travis could not believe what he was hearing. Travis felt sheer joy because his parents were giving him this opportunity to go to a different country and visit his old friends.

Once he arrived in London and settled into his room, Travis set out towards the city. He started out walking the streets, taking in all the amazing sights, including the incredible architecture of some of the buildings. After walking around for several hours, Travis decided to go into some of the different buildings. Later that day, Travis called his friends, Jimmy and Brandon, to see if they were free that night to hang out. Travis was glad to hear that they could, so he decided to go back to his hotel room and get ready for the night. He got ready in casual attire and set out. Travis told Jimmy and Brandon that they should meet at the local fair that was taking place that night. He took a taxi to the fairgrounds and was utterly excited to have fun with his old friends.

Travis met up with Jimmy and Brandon, and they had loads of fun. They talked about what was new in their lives. Travis told them how he just graduated from Vanderbilt University with a degree in psychology. He also mentioned how his parents gave him this opportunity to come to England. Then, Brandon told Travis how he graduated with a degree in medicine one year prior. Jimmy described how he was still in college at one of the local universities in town, and he was studying business. At the fair, the group of friends had fun, enjoying the rides and good food. Travis then asked them if they were free the following night for dinner, but they weren't. However, Jimmy and Brandon were both free two days from then, so they set aside that night for dinner and made reservations. Travis then said goodbye and returned to his hotel. He determined that he would tour the city more the next day.

The following morning, Travis set out to tour London. He decided to go into the different shops and stores to see what the city sold. Travis came out of the shops with several different souvenirs. Travis then had lunch at a local cafe with an assortment of foods. After lunch, he went to the Natural History Museum and the National Gallery museum. Travis was intrigued by the history of the country, and he enjoyed visiting and seeing the museums. Later that day, Travis had dinner and returned to his hotel exhausted. However, he was looking forward to hanging out with friends again.

The next day, it was raining when Travis woke up, so he decided to go to the Chelsea Club Museum and spend the day there until dinner. This museum specifically told about the history of Chelsea Club soccer team. This was by far his favorite museum because he was interested in soccer, the country's sport . Then at about 6:00 PM, Travis took a taxi to a nearby restaurant to meet up with Jimmy and Brandon for dinner. Upon arriving, he discovered that Jimmy and Brandon were already there. They all greeted each other happily, and they were glad they were getting the opportunity to hang out again. They were seated and began talking, mostly about how college was for each of them. The group then got their food and began indulging in delicious steak and salad. However, during dinner, Travis felt that something was amiss.

When he looked behind him, Travis did in fact see two anonymous men in black suits looking his way, but they quickly turned their heads when Travis looked back. Travis was curious as to why these strange men were watching him eat, and he got a sense that it wasn't good. He told Jimmy and Brandon of his suspicions, and they all came to an agreement that it would be best to leave. So the group of guys got up and left the restaurant, and they piled into a taxi to go back to Travis' hotel. After driving a few miles, Travis looked back and discovered that a black sedan was following them with the same two men inside! Travis was starting to get apprehensive as to what might happen. His friends agreed that it was odd. Travis knew he was in a tough position.

Travis told the cab driver to take several turns to try to lose the car. It became apparent and inevitable that the men were on to him. These actions proved to be unsuccessful. Travis ultimately decided to consult with his parents and see if they could provide insight as to why there were people following him. During the conversation, Travis's father described a time in his life about 3 years before where he had adversaries because of certain circumstances. He explained that he beat out two men for the most important job at his company, and they were upset about it for weeks. They abhorred him. After that happened, his father told Travis that he received threats that included the men knowing information about his family. His father then proposed an idea to Travis: a way he could lose them by stopping a block away from his hotel and running from there to his room. Travis had to contemplate what to do, but he decided to follow his father's sage advice. After about another 10 minutes of driving, Travis arrived at the hotel. He knew that he would have to run fast to not get captured by the two men.

Travis immediately got out of the taxi with Jimmy and Brandon, and they sprinted toward his hotel. He looked back and saw that the men were indeed following him. Travis reached the lobby of the hotel and saw that he had a good lead on the two men. He reached the elevator in the hotel and had a considerable lead, which meant that he lost them for the time being. Travis then went up to his room with his friends and called the police. A few minutes after calling the police, they arrived at the hotel, and Travis looked out the window to see the police taking the men away. Although it was a serious situation, he was glad that the men were taken away. Jimmy and Brandon then decided to leave because of the whole situation. However, they thanked Travis for hanging out with them. It was a long and eventful night for Travis. Unfortunately, he later learned that the two men were not being charged with anything.

Incidentally, Travis decided to return home the next day. He called his parents to tell them that he was fine, and he was returning home because of the events that occurred the previous night. For Travis, it was definitely a remarkable trip. Overall, Travis had an exhilarating time, and he enjoyed hanging out with his friends.

m
GARDNER

I was fifteen years old was when I figured out what I would do for the next part of my frantic and erratic life. My name is Angelina Dafter, but everyone calls me Angel. I am 40 years old now, but at the age of fifteen, I found out what kind of unpredictable lifestyle I would live for the next 50 years of my life. I hope this story is as inspiring to you as it is to me.

Back then, my parents thought that since I hadn't seen my aunt and uncle for almost 4 years, that it would be good idea to visit them on the family farm in Kansas. I was sent on an airplane, by myself, for the first time in my life, and I hoped it would be as exhilarating as I had imagined to see my family. As I boarded the plane, I observed some remarkably distinct people. All of the men on the plane were wearing austere black suits and dark shades, but one stuck out to me because of his strangely shaped black beard. All of the women were dressed in dingy clothing, but they also had perfectly pampered pink manicured nails that seemed almost impossible to overlook. The four hour flight was, to my bewilderment, quite pleasant. At first, I was nervous to go on a plane by myself and thought that I would be bored, but I ended up watching an interesting movie and ate peanuts. I exited the plane and waited in the airport for my aunt and uncle to pick me up. After 30 minutes of waiting, I got an inconvenient text message stating that my aunt and uncle were unable to come get me from the airport. I took matters into my own hands and decided to take a cab to the family farm.

I ran around for almost an hour trying to find a cab driver. I finally found a nice man to take me. About 10 minutes into the ride, I realized I didn't know the directions to the farm or have the money to pay for the ride. I leaned forward to tell the driver, but he refused to help me, and then the cab came to an abrupt stop. The next thing I knew, the cab began to fill with some gas that made me feel strangely tired. My fervent endeavor to unlock and open the door and escape was unsuccessful…

When I woke up, I looked around but was unable to see anything. Wherever I was… it was pitch black. I began to think of the things I remembered. I was in Kansas, going to visit my aunt and uncle. I flew here by myself on a four hour flight, and I had taken a cab. Wait, the cab driver was on the plane; he was the one with the strange black beard! In the cab, he hadn't been in his suit though, rather, he had on overalls, but he was there. Could he have anything to do with where I was? Just then, a light flashed on, and a door began to open. I stared at the hand that reached out to me. It had pink nail polish, just like the ladies that were on the plane.

"Hello Angel, do you have any idea where you are or what has happened?" said a woman named Debra

Fisher. I had recognized her from a get-together last summer.

I thought about the observations I had made so far and tried to take some control of the situation.

"No ma'am," I replied, trying to sound less tremulous than I felt.

She began to tell me that I had been taken by a group of FBI agents. My aunt and uncle had been taken away by someone, and this group was on their case. They had identified a suspect named David Davis. The problem was that he already knew all of the agents on that team. They needed me to catch him or render him helpless.

"Why do you need me to do it?" I questioned.

"Because, sweetie, the suspect shouldn't be able to recognize you, and we think that you have the potential to go unnoticed in a larger crowd of people. Just don't slip up," she answered with a wink.

Of course, I wasn't going to refuse helping a federal service, not after they admitted that they believed in me. First, they needed to disguise me, because it was standard procedure. They changed my clothes, dyed my hair, and did my makeup. After careful observation, they had memorized David's daily routines, of course until he left his work office. Once I was ready to go out, they took me to the place he ate lunch every day. It was a quiet and small restaurant, and all of the workers seemed to recognize him. I silently observed him eat his lunch and followed him out of the building.

The next place he went to was the local carnival. He rode the Ferris wheel twice and the swings once. Then he got a corn dog. I was in the line behind him, hoping that he wouldn't notice. Unfortunately when I sneezed, he turned around and took off. He threw the corn dog in a red trash can near the exit and the chase began. We ran four blocks southeast and turned left many times. Eventually we ran into a dead end, and he turned around. There was a moment when I thought that my job was complete. Then as soon as that moment left my mind and I was going to get him, an ear shattering noise rang in my ears. A bomb exploded that was bigger than any I had ever seen in any movie. We both flew to opposites sides of the alley.

When I woke up next, I was in a hospital room staring at my parents, my aunt, and my uncle in the eye. They all seemed calm, given the situation I had been in. My mother then told me that she, my father, my aunt, and my uncle were all agents as well and that was the reason they put so much trust in me with this case. After that, a doctor came in and told me that I had broken my right leg and arm. I was going to gain full function back with rest and rehab. My family went to eat lunch so that the agents could come to speak with me. They were amazed at the progress I had made in such a short time. But they were concerned with the decisions I made that could've gotten me killed, not to mention killed many other people. However, they, well I, did catch the suspect. He was keeping my aunt and uncle in a shed 5 miles away from the FBI headquarters in Kansas. David was arrested and thrown in prison for life.

"Debra, what about the bomb? Who set it?" I asked.

"We did. That may sound weird, but without it he would have gotten away and we couldn't let that happen," she replied.

The agency decided to grant me a full time job with them. A job that would define my life and the way that I decided to live it. I enjoyed every minute of my job, and to this day, I still do. The best decision I made in my life was joining that team because they became not only my coworkers, but my family. They have changed my life in ways that nothing else could. If you get a chance to do something irrational or crazy, take it. It could be the best thing that will ever happen to you.

GILLBREATHE
I am a Fish

"What do we got?" Detective Cod inquired.

"It looks like some erratic psychofish destroyed the housing at the Winslow Reef with the intention of getting back at a rival school. It sure subjected the citizens of the reef to a lot of sheer agony, so much I can hardly help but wince at the fact that there is someone that utterly scathing in all of the sea, that they can't see the significance of destroying the Reef. We shouldn't neglect that fact," I explained, appalled at the fact that this could happen to our reef.

"Do we have any leads, or any evidence, that's still intact? Something that might reveal who did this?" Cod asked.

"Well, remarkably, we do. Like here where the criminal seems to have shed his angler mask, which is bewildering that such a worthy adversary would leave that kind of evidence behind. Also there are some scales over here. The way the scales overlap and the shape is confirmation that we are looking for a flounder about 18 or 19 inches long and about 4 pounds," I deduced fervently while the others listened.

"Have you considered the chance that there is an overshark behind this. That someone lower down, no more than a prawn, carried it out?" Cod questioned condescendingly.

"Sure, it's a possibility, but I am hesitant to think so, because we would have been able to tell that from the considerably more than cursory search we did. I mean, we did this methodically, not just randomly," I rebuffed. "If you want though, we will be obedient to your request and hasten to cast this evidence out to be analyzed by more 'competent' analysts, so they can trace the eccentric who did this, and make sure we didn't overlook something. How does that sound?"

"That sounds great, especially under the circumstances, plus it can never hurt to consult an expert on important cases like this."

What does Cod take me for? Some irrational, second rate carp? I personally feel that he's the one who's considerably more incompetent in this partnership. I really hate to show such scorn towards him, but he deserves it. I mean, I am the fish who studied scale printing, fish justice, psyfishology, and fishenomics at EAC. I am also the fish who won the Nibble Fish Peace Prize for my assistance in the capture of the famous coral thief Sauger Sábalo. I was also the fish who beat Jack Dempsey in a boxing match, in the first round. That was ME, Sillago Devario. All of those exhilarating times were me! What has Cod done that is so special? He barely graduated from ECC, a clearly inferior school to EAC.

He still lives in his parents' anemone, because he can't afford his own. And all he does now is feed off my success like a pilot fish does to a shark.

I have had a revelation, after much meditation, contemplation, and the expenditure of much time. I don't even need Cod; he's not a vital part of my life. On the contrary, he is a distinctly and invariably unwanted presence that is really just intruding on my space. He will inevitably take away all the affection left in me, until I am sodden in the dingy weariness that alienates me from fishanity. Then some poor fish will be tasked with the singularly most precarious task of retrieving the last remnant of me from the sadness and depression of the abyss and restoring me to the bleak ocean I used to live in. After the initial consternation I will feel after being laboriously brought out of the abyss, I will resume my hatred of Cod.

See, I have always been an upright fish, but I don't mind changing that if it means I don't have to be plunged into the remoteness of the abyss and then summoned back. I won't let that happen. In fact, I will kill Cod before letting it happen. I've always considered killing him for his ignorance and arrogance, but never actually took it seriously. It was so persistently occurring that I got used to it. But now I am realizing that I have to act on it or go insane.

"Sure thing, boss," I said with a customary sardonic look on my face, "But first, one thing."

"What?"

"This."

The hook sank into his gills, deeper, then deeper; he muttered a "Why?" then was dead. I couldn't help but feel an overwhelming sense of relief. A relief that could not be matched by anything. I was free at last.

b
GOLDEN
Dil Howlter

You see, it was the perfect day: the sky was drizzling rain the temperature of the Antarctic region, and the grey clouds overlooked the bustling city like a suffocating blanket. The most exciting and wonderful part of it, though, was that my Internet connection was back after two weeks on hiatus, as I was moving to London with my affable boyfriend, Phil. Two whole weeks without Internet can really change a person for the worse, especially when you make your living from it.

"Dan, where did you put the box of dishes? The kitchen?" Phil called from the other room, obviously frustrated with my organizational skills. After a few minutes of crashing into things and muffled sounds of delight, he waltzed into the room with a giant stuffed anime character and plopped himself on the ground, pulling me into a tight hug in the process. He smiled at me, his pale blue eyes looking directly into mine as our fingers interlaced.

Phil. He is like a 5-year-old child with the body of a 20-something-year-old man. He has a miniature, stuffed lion that he constantly has perched on his shoulder, and he is always clad in one of his brightly-colored, nerdy t-shirts and mismatching socks. We had been dating for a few years after I met him online. We had found a mutual interest in creating both gaming and anecdotal videos for the internet, making us the perfect pair.

"They're in the kitchen, Phillip," I said in confirmation, enunciating both syllables of his name, which he hated with the passion of a thousand fiery suns. He scowled playfully at me and, when he tried to get up, he fell on top of me, his lanky frame crashing into my own. I ruffled his bangs and smiled teasingly at his clumsiness. "You idiot," I laughed, a smile stretching from ear to ear on both of our faces. His eyes crinkle in the cutest way before we both get up to unpack, ready to begin a new video for this week.

Recently, we had been hearing a lot about an online game called the *Grims*. From what I'd found from the Internet, it is a virtual world in which you make characters and control them, giving them depressing lives and such. It became very popular, so we decided to check it out and post a video to our page. This was definitely going to be interesting.

"Hello, Internet," I began confidently with a smirk. This usually is the best way to start off a video, according to the subscribers to our channel. I waited for a moment until Phil hopped into the frame, a grin plastered on his face.

"Hiiiii!" Phil chimed in happily, smiling like a small child as he did so... He was so adorable... "So *Daniel*, what shall we be doing today?" We began to explain what we were doing, and we created a character named

Dil Howlter, as a combination of our names: Dan Howell and Phil Lester. Out of the blue, he kissed my cheek and I blushed profusely, smiling like a schoolboy. He muttered a soft, "I love you," before we continued. You see, this is why we edit our videos. Our fans already wanted us together, so if they found out about our relationship, we'd be dead men.

*   *   *

Well, it had been about a month since we created Dil, and it has been a hit with the Web, so we continued for the time being. This whole thing has been fun, but I think our computer had started acting up. Dil Howlter wouldn't do some of the simple things we make him do, such as "walk" where we controlled him. Likewise, the game would glitch out every now and then, randomly shutting down the program. I surmised it to be a problem with the drivers or something of the sort. A cryptic text box with nothing but symbols and other emoticons appeared earlier, but Phil and I couldn't figure it out. When we tried to close the pop-up, the screen was covered in flashing, multicolored dots along with every other device in the house, including the television, our phones, and the other laptop. A few muffled words that we couldn't understand came through the speakers, then everything went black and stopped. We didn't know what was wrong; maybe the fuse box was acting up or something? We thought about discontinuing the *Grims* videos, but they're too popular. Maybe we need to get a new laptop...

b. golden

*   *   *

Translation of text box:

"Greetings. My name is Dil Howlter. I cannot
communicate in the way that a normal human being
can. We speak in Grimilish, a language of shrieks and
growls not known to any human being, yet we can still
translate your language into ours. We have no control
over our actions or words, which come as the Masters
command us. However, we have found a virus, which
is located in our database. A virus which will leave any
device on which our lives are tampered with subject to
scathing consequences. It was located through a glitch
in our system which allows us to move on our own and
have control. In more human-like terms, we will be
freed from this prison. Forever."

*   *   *

Our computer just glitched really bad. It completely shut
down and erased all of our files for the next video. It's
been acting strangely ever since we made Dil. Maybe the
hard drive can't handle all of this memory... or so we
thought. Dil won't even do the simplest of things now,
like walking or sleeping. He is beginning to speak in
English, saying random things like "erase" and "delete."
We contacted the company that makes the game, but we
haven't heard back from them. The company has
apparently been on leave for an "interminable amount of
time." This is beginning to feel weird.

"Hey babe," I heard as Phil opened the door to our apartment. He sat down next to me with an adorably cheesy grin on his face. "So how's the laptop situation, Dan?" he asked, sobering at the thought of losing the only source of income we have, not to mention all of the data we need for our videos. He cuddled closer, holding my hand and staring at the laptop. As I pulled it out of the case, I saw all of the newfound cat stickers Phil had placed all over its cover. Seeing my glare, he hoarsely mumbled, "It *improves* it..." and scrunched his face up like an indignant child.

I succumbed to his adorably frustrated look, and we both laughed, basking in the glow of each other. After a few hours of television watching and a cup of coffee, we sat back down, much closer this time. After a bit of deciding what to do, we continued to play the *Grims*, if it'll cooperate. This time, we were trying to renovate our Grim's poorly constructed virtual house and finish another Dil Howlter video.

*   *   *

We have found a way in. It all falls tonight. -D.H.

*   *   *

The very next evening, as Phil and I came home from a wonderful night out, we sat down in our huge bean bag chair, ready to go settle down, hold hands, and maybe watch a geeky film. However, the time soon turned from midnight to 4 a.m. and we decided to browse the

Internet, if the stupid laptop would turn on. Seeing as this was a rare occurrence now because of the technical difficulties, we weren't hopeful. He ruffled my hair, a short, dark fringe, and cuddled closer, his head resting on my shoulder. He came even closer, pulling a blanket over us to derive any heat from the room, as it was freezing in the little, austere apartment. We heard a notification coming from the laptop case in the corner. I got up, much to my boyfriend's chagrin, and retrieved it from the floor. Trying to gingerly endeavor to turn on the computer without breaking it, I finally got it on.

Grimacing at the sudden brightness, we stared as an animated face came up on the screen. It was a gruesome representation of Dil Howlter, his face askew and seemingly broken. My horrified partner and I stared at the screen as if it were a dead animal lying on the ground. The screen suddenly cracked, a bright shower of sparks drifted onto the beanbag chair. We screamed simultaneously as the computer flickered on and off. Through this, though, the face on the screen seemed very calm and spoke only these words in a horrifying, digital voice:

"Greetings. My name is Dil Howlter. We have come."

And, with a sound like thousands of voices screaming in unison, the computer crashed, leaving us in total darkness.

HAMBLIN

Hammy, The Best Writer Ever

Mr. Wilson boarded the passenger plane he was going to take to Detroit, Michigan. He had his Wireless Beats Studios on and was jamming to Wiz Khalifa's "Black and Yellow." When he casually sat down in his seat, Wiz's verse was, "black stripe, yellow paint, them haters scared of it, but them bros ain't" (Wiz Khalifa, "Black and Yellow"). He put his bag down hesitantly because of the dingy floor, and he grabbed his laminated folder titled "1-2 period English" to start grading papers. He reached for his green pen in his satchel, but he couldn't find it. He began frantically searching his satchel, for he HAD to have his green pen; his green pens were a part of his soul. He reached into the side compartment and located one, but when he yanked the pen out, it was red! Mr. Wilson thought to himself, "As much as I hate to say this, it will have to do."

He read the first sentence of Jay's paper, about the growing affection between two students in the class, but suddenly an intruder, carrying a pistol at her side, stood up from her seat and told everybody to be quiet. The woman rushed to the front of the plane to make sure she could see everybody and that they weren't doing anything suspicious.

The intruder was trying to cause harm, the people assumed because of the look on her face. Suddenly, Mr. Wilson stood up from his seat and shouted, "To Infinity and Beyond!" Nothing happened. Mr. Wilson was panicking because he was going to summon his super powers to beat the intruder into tiny, little remnants, but of course, he didn't have any super powers.

He had to improvise. He rushed up to the intruder and tried to stop her, but the hijacker pulled out a gun, and Mr. Wilson stopped in his tracks. Mr. Wilson moved up and down to try to play with the bad guy's brain, but he only fatigued himself. He thought to himself, *To get out of this situation I need to pull out my pen and push that top until it pops*. When he did that, the pen turned into a sword instead of a writing utensil, as he was expecting. This intimidated the intruder, and she fired a frantic shot at Mr. Wilson. The shot deflected off of Mr. Wilson's sword and hit the orange, 4-inch, door hinge to the left of them. The criminal, with a scornful look on her face, fired four more scoring bullets at Mr. Wilson. He erratically dodged all four of them and stabbed the intruder right in the heart. Everybody on the plane cheered for him.

Mr. Wilson had expended all of his energy fighting off the bad guy, but then he remembered he had the best writer ever in his class, Hammy! He immediately ran to his seat and pulled out his laminated folder and flipped to Hammy's narrative. He began to read, "Mr. Wilson boarded the passenger plane…"

HARPER
Gleipnir

It was early in the morning, just after first light, and the hooves of horses pulling carts on the cobblestone path through town could already be heard. The remote town existed on the outskirts of deep and scarcely explored forest lands. The local caravan was departing, and a young blacksmith's son was bidding farewell to his parents. He was a boy no older than fourteen, with scraggly, light hair and eyes the color of fresh spring leaves. His father occasionally went on the arduously long trips with the caravans in an attempt to sell his fabricated iron goods. However, this time his wife would accompany him. She was going in an attempt to earn more income, as her weaving skills had recently proved to be an easy source of it; her elegant works could not be overlooked by any buyer. As their son, Fenrir, was thin and frail, he was deemed too weak to make the trip with them; he would be staying behind to look over their home and shop, much to his utter dismay. The night prior to the caravan's departure, Fenrir had displayed this by fervently protesting to his predicament until his voice had grown hoarse.

Fenrir poked at his self-made meal of stew with a wooden spoon. It was later in the day, long after the caravan had departed. Despite the effort he'd put into it, the stew was neglected and had already lost its warmth. Fenrir was reluctant to eat, fearing he would only regurgitate the food – a bad case of nausea had set upon him, and his stomach felt like a foul witch's cauldron. Fenrir did not see this as an indication of illness. Rather, he dismissively reassured himself that he was fine, and he regarded it as a mere side effect of loneliness. He tended to feel that way when he was alone, after all, so he saw no reason in being worried. Abandoning his cold, untouched stew, Fenrir quietly stood up from his chair and walked towards the door to begin his daily tasks. Suddenly, he came to a halt, one hand clutching his stomach. The ill feeling had turned to scathing pain, and a sense of fear washed over him. He had heard of this feeling before, hadn't he?

Fenrir recalled rumors that had been going around – rumors about this kind of pain, and how it led to things far more sinister if left to progress. The town courier had called it lycanthropy, the terrible affliction of beast-men. Fenrir thought he was stupid for even considering such a possibility, but… What if this really was such a thing? He hesitantly grabbed ahold of the hilt of his father's iron sword. He was quite safe in the caravan without it, and had left it for his son. He had made it apparent Fenrir needed to take it with him if he even considered leaving the village – it could be quite dangerous in the forest, so it was mad not to bring protection. Fenrir doubted he should make such a big deal about it, and he was reluctant to take the sword with him. Despite his doubts, he grabbed his satchel, which could store a few essentials if he needed them, and raced out the door with the sword at his side. All the while, he tried to ignore the aches and pains in his stomach.

Fenrir honestly hoped the help he sought would be worth it. He had dashed out of town, down the forest trail on a journey towards help. After two hours of exhaustion and agonizing pain, he finally arrived at his destination. By then, the pain had grown immense, but he did his best to ignore it as he approached the small camp ahead. It belonged to the medicine man of the woods, whom could hopefully identify what was plaguing poor Fenrir. After Fenrir had called out, a tall, ragged-looking fellow emerged from the large teepee in the center of the camp. He avoided eye contact with Fenrir, who didn't hesitate to explain his presence and what he needed of the doctor. The individual, who Fenrir assumed was the one he was looking for, remained motionless for a few seconds longer before going back into the teepee. Fenrir was confused at his silence, and was even more so when the medicine man returned with a piece of parchment about five minutes later.

"...Uh... If you don't mind me asking, what exactly is this...?" Fenrir asked. His stomach growled, a little painfully, almost as if it were asking the same. The medicine man remained silent, and Fenrir had to ask again before he finally spoke.

"This is what you need," he said, as if it were obvious. "You *are* afflicted, so you need to gather these items."

His words made Fenrir's heart sink in dismay, and he focused on the parchment, reading over the list that was etched upon it with ink.

"Why? Is it a recipe for the cure?" Fenrir asked, hoping it was that or at least something of that nature. He hated the awful pain in his gut and wanted this plague remedied. The medicine man could do that, couldn't he? After all, the only reason Fenrir had known about him was due to his medical successes.

"…No. There is no such thing. This serum will merely dull the effects. It is all I can provide to you," said the medicine man shortly, who still didn't dare to look Fenrir in the eye. Fenrir felt the claws of fear once again, increasing the pain in his stomach. If the medicine man could only dull this disease, then just what sort of effect would it have on Fenrir? Would he really turn into something out of a nightmare?

With his stomach still aching, Fenrir continued down the forest path, examining the list on the parchment. Two of the three ingredients would be easy enough, he guessed. The recipe called for Gloamgrass bud and Louta nut, which were common in these forests. However, the third was the claw of a bear, and Fenrir shuddered at the thought of facing one. Shoving it from his mind, Fenrir gazed around as he walked. If he paid attention, he would see if there were any Gloamgrass stalks or Louta nut trees growing around the path. Since they were common, the bright bluish green stalk of a Gloamgrass plant was soon visible among the roots of a tree. Feeling delighted at the quick success, Fenrir dashed over, slicing off one of the buds in an almost careless fashion with his sword. *Maybe this will be faster than I thought,* Fenrir thought to himself as he put the bud into his satchel. *I bet I could find a bear's claw just lying around at this rate!* Even the pain in his stomach dulled slightly as hope glowed within him.

Fenrir shuffled around the undergrowth, leaving the path to examine the branches of the nearby trees. The tree he had discovered the Gloamgrass under hadn't provided him the other necessary ingredient, but he continued on to search. Eventually, Fenrir spotted the dusky-brown nuts among the branches of a pitifully flimsy tree and found no trouble in simply bending the thin trunk to where he could reach them. After grabbing a few, Fenrir released the tree, which snapped back like a whip. He then placed the Louta nuts with the Gloamgrass bud in his satchel, dreading the final step that loomed before him. *How am I supposed to find a bear's claw?* Fenrir thought, hoping he *could* find one just lying around, like he had hoped at earlier. His aching stomach seemed to worsen a little, too, creating a storm of fear that began to set over his brain.

Fenrir ventured deeper into the woods, where the predators would be. He was met with trouble in the form of bear tracks – bears were supposed to be common here, but Fenrir was utterly terrified. He was about to run, ready to give up, but froze when he spotted a large, dark shape ahead of him. It was most definitely a bear! Fenrir stood stiller than a statue as the bear chuffed threateningly, and he could already imagine his fate. He really hadn't thought this through, had he? Now, staring into the agape jaws of the creature, he could feel fear holding him in place.

With his fear, Fenrir could feel that awful, cursed pain rising up through him, to the point he wanted to keel over. Forget stomach pain, his whole body was screaming at him in agony! Before Fenrir could wonder what on Earth was happening to him, the ground was coming up underneath him – he was falling, *fainting!* His fear peaked when he hit the ground, wondering if he would ever get up again. The pain became too much to endure, and as he stared in terror at the approaching bear, the world proceeded to go dark around him. The wave of dizzying blackness pushed consciousness from him, and the last thing he saw before he went out was the sudden look of fear that crossed the face of the animal before him.

It was not until hours after the incident that Fenrir groggily awoke from his slumber and sat up, bringing a hand to his head. It took him a minute to realize he wasn't where he'd previously been – in fact, he found himself back at the medicine man's camp. Fenrir cast a glance around, eyes stretched wide with confusion.

"Uh… Hello?" Fenrir called out, struck dumb. No answer. Then, he saw the medicine man, who was dashing towards his teepee. "Wait, Sir-!" Fenrir exclaimed, but the man disappeared into it – only to return with a vial. "What's that? What's going on? How did I get here?" Fenrir pressed, but the medicine man merely shook his head and held out the vial. "Is this-?" Fenrir began, but didn't continue when the man merely nodded. Fenrir was utterly bewildered by him. Hadn't a bear's claw been required for this serum? Did that mean the bear was dead? Had the medicine man killed it? How on Earth had he gotten there? He had many other questions he wanted to ask, and opened his mouth to do so, but the man was herding him out of his camp already! "Hold on! What do I do with this?" Fenrir managed to choke out as he was being pushed out, frustrated at the man's silence.

"You drink it. Now go, go. Get on out. You're trouble," the medicine man snapped, and Fenrir, taken aback by the hostility, blinked in a dumb, confused fashion before turning around to leave. Fenrir didn't want to spend another moment around the eccentric, and he shook his head with a grumble as he ran back for the trail, stuffing the vial into his satchel hastily. *That was too weird! It's like I teleported!* Fenrir thought in confusion, recalling the face-off with the bear. *And he was acting so strange, too! I don't even want to know what happened.... At least it's over, though,* Fenrir thought, relief washing over him as he ran. However, he could feel an odd sensation behind him, and he halted, feeling cautious. Was it another predator, like the bear from before? Fenrir looked over his shoulder, paranoid, and didn't see anything... At first, that is. Much to his awe, though, he suddenly noticed what had caused the sensation. Below his waist, there was a fur-covered, chestnut-colored, wolfish *tail* sticking out behind him! Fenrir shook his head, trying to convince himself he was only seeing things, but the tail remained, waving innocently. How was he going to explain *this* to his parents? He didn't expect them to react well... With a frustrated sigh, Fenrir shook his head, and looked ahead of him once more. *Why did this have to happen to me?* he thought with a groan, beginning his long trek home.

HATCH
Greed and Grief

Phil was an ordinary person. On weekdays he got up and went to work. On weekends, he stayed at home and lives quietly, like everyone else. Yes, he was just like everyone else: almost nothing he did at all deviated from what everyone considered normal behavior. However, one aspect of his life was incredibly different: he had a pet unicorn named Sleipnir. He found and befriended this incredibly rare creature on a hunting trip. One day as he was making breakfast, he switched on the T.V., which was on the counter opposite from him. It was on the news channel, and the current story grabbed his interest. "Eccentric millionaires from all over the globe are having a competition to find who has the rarest and most expensive clothes; they're all searching for new materials," the newscaster said. Sleipnir walked into the room, and stood in front of the T.V., And, for a brief second, Phil considered something bewildering, but almost immediately dismissed the idea, and was suddenly fascinated by the buttons on his coat. A commercial break started, and Phil noticed all of the advertisements offering grand rewards.

"C'mon Nir, time for a walk," he said. Sleipnir trotted over obediently, and they walked out together. Phil looked again at Sleipnir's elegant mane, and once again, the thought came to him, and he winced at the depravity his mind could produce; it was quite disconcerting at times. He couldn't imagine doing anything cruel to his most intimate friend, who had been a part of his life for years. They continued their stroll in silence. After several years of living in their normal urban community; people weren't shocked to see a unicorn accompanying him.

When they got home, they were surprised to see Axiam, one of the richest people in the country. He'd sent agents all over the globe, searching for the rarest animal, to use its hide for a material. When they came back with reports of a unicorn with glistening coat, and he had to confirm these weren't fabrications. Axiam said, "That is an exquisite coat. I will have it: name your price."

"I'm sorry sir," Phil said, "I won't let you take Sleipnir, not for any amount of money."

"Ah, so then what is it you want? Fame? Power? I am quite an influential man as you undoubtedly know."

Phil considered the implications of this offer, and what he could do with that power. He slowly shook his head; however it was clear his resolve was wavering.

"You see, everyone has their price" Axiam said.

"Offer me money, power, and everything I want," Phil said hesitantly.

"All I have and more, for the beast."

"Deal," he said, feeling exhilarated, already thinking of what he could do with this wealth.

Sleipnir looked sadly at Phil as if he knew his fate as they carted him away. Strangely, Phil felt little remorse. The years went on, Axiam winning even more money from the competition. Phil had it all: money, power, friends. After a night of partying with his "rich" and "proper" friends, he was back at his mansion, fifty separate rooms, yet all empty. He had all he wanted: fame, power, friends, and yet continued to wonder what he was missing. He walked over to his expensive closet, took off his luxurious and rare suit jacket and, just as he was about to hang it up with the others, he let it drop to the floor. He slowly turned and looked at it and wondered what he had become. How long ago had he shed his humanity, he fit perfectly into an imperfect world. He tried to control his life by bargaining it away. He unwittingly traded all that made him human for material gain.

He stood and stared at the jacket on the floor, only thinking of that one question: How long? How long have humans tried to idealize certain qualities, make the perfect personality? He had tried to make himself perfect by bartering for power, fame, and wealth. How long ago was individualism lost? For how long have we existed, thinking of the lesser things in life, while ignoring all that makes a person human? Are we human? Are we not savages, fearing change, rejecting all that doesn't "fit in"? Have we tried to make the puzzle pieces fit together by sanding the edges so much, that all the edges are no longer perceivable as separate?

As he stood there, staring at the jacket, he wondered if he truly ever cared about anything other than being accepted. The deformed are cast out, ignored, and shamed, while those who conceal their deformities are considered superior, rather than lowly cowards. How many people are content to be still faces in a stagnant crowd? Why do we have a natural fear of change? The answers all became clear to Phil then. Humans fear change because it threatens their place in the established order. No-one is willing to take risks, to stand out, or to be different. We're running in circles, chasing progress and making huge leaps backwards. One man said, "Look here! I have found the end!" and the others laugh at him and say "Mad fool! That is the beginning; we are far ahead of that!"

Phil realized how wrong he had been about his greatness; he was the lowest of cowards, the most shameful type of person. Seeking to improve himself; instead he became something other than himself, with no remorse, individualism, or anything other than what others wanted him to be. He tried to become popular, but succeeded in merely hiding himself behind a wall of others, hiding everything different and unique about himself. For the first time, Phil wept for Sleipnir. He saw the blindness of his actions and realized his ignorance. He was appalled by this revelation, and vowed to travel the world, speaking on everything he learned, so others wouldn't fall into the same trap as he had so foolishly done.

wilson
HIGGS
Life of a Prisoner

Prison is a damp, dreary, and dingy place. There's little contact with the outside world. I have been here for only one day, and it feels like a million years. I feel like it was inevitable that I would try and escape. If I failed, then I would be sent to I.S.O. I.S.O is short for isolation, and if you were one of the unlucky few to be sent there, you would emaciated. It will drive you mad in just two days, so mad that you can plead release based on insanity. This happened to people because they misbehaved or because the warden or guards didn't like them. There was no one there who was willing to risk it, no one except me. First, I needed some powerful allies, but I was having trouble getting into a gang till I met Rose Reina Rebecca who is a girl.

She is one of the most popular prisoners; she was like the queen bee of the prison. At first, she tried to conceal our friendship. We did this because it would not look good for Rose if he was seen with a new prisoner. After over four years of hiding the friendship, the whole prison discovered our secret, but it was ok that everyone found out. I was not the new prisoner anymore as I had learned the ropes of prison. I now know how to avoid getting beat up and who was king of the prison.

Rose and I had started the toughest prison gang called The Smashers. We were the toughest gang on the whole prison. We had Destructive Doug, Danny the Destroyer, Domino the Delicate, me, Radiant Rose, and John the Joke. We all hated the prison and needed to get out, so we made a risky plan to escape. If this didn't work, then we would all go to I.S.O.

The plan was that Doug, Danny, and Domino were going to distract the guards while Rose, John, and I make dummies to convince the guard that we are asleep. While the dummies are doing their job, we will escape through a sewage pipe ,that we discovered a month ago in the kitchen where I had lunch duty that week. We would finally become free. We had a week to prepare for the escape and get the supplies for the dummies. This part of the plan was due to poor planning, my friend would give us the stuff on the next truck supply stop at the prison. The next delivery was a week before our escape and we could not move the date back. Yet we had to because John was being moved to another prison in about a week and one day. I told my friend we needed pillow mannequin heads, a speaker, and recording devices. I hoped my friend was meticulous in choosing the items he sent us to make the dummies.

The night of the escape came, and we did not forget anything. The night was perfect: the clouds were blocking out the moon, making it extremely dark outside. We sent out the boys to distract the guard while we got ready. When the dummies were set up and put in place, we went for the sewage pipe and went down it. As we all got down, the alarms went off. They must have discovered our decoys and set off the alarm.

We sprinted for the exit and what felt like miles of pipe took us hours to go through. All of a sudden, we saw at the end of the tunnel were some bars. We were frantic. As we reached the end, we saw the bars on the exit. they were not there when we checked it out the week before. We were pushing on the bars with all of our strength, but nothing worked. We all heard voices and barking coming closer and closer and closer. To our relief, a policeman came to the outside of the bars. He looked inside was about let his dog sniff for us, but before he did he must have heard a noise and left. We all breathed a sigh of relief and began pushing on it again. We waited for him to come back, but he never did. We kept pushing, but the bar never broke. John suddenly told the group that he had a bar cutter, and we all about strangled him. We cut the bar and climbed out. We ran and ran and ran as far as we could, then when we were far enough away from the prison, we split up. Rose stayed with me, though, we moved to Canada together.

We lived happily together for over fifty years, where Rose and I had children and we lived very happy lives. That is, until Rose became homesick: she wanted to see the states again. We decided to go back. When we got to the border, we found that the police were still looking for us. We were on the FBI's Top Ten Most Wanted List. We were apparently blamed for the escape of all the criminals in the prison. The border officer took one look at us and immediately recognized us. I later asked him how he recognized us. He told me we were the reason he was not warden of that prison, and we cost him his job. We recognized him too: it was the policemen who looked in the sewage pipe and almost caught us. He grabbed Rose and I and threw us in jail, where we served our thirty years.

jacob
HOWARD
Truth about Teachers

The lights suddenly flickered and then there was darkness. Richard was lost in a world he had never explored. He had been dared to spend the night at school, which, for a fourth grader, would make him a king. All he had to do was make it through the night. So here he was, trapped in the third stall of the boy's bathroom, becoming a legend. How hard could this be?

Richard has been stuck in the dingy landfill of a bathroom that had been overflowing with paper towels and other trash for as long as anyone could remember, and naturally he drifted off to sleep. Suddenly, he was awoken by what he surmised could only be the sounds of copy machine. He was intrigued and drawn out of the bathroom to find out what mysterious object had made the screeching noises.

He was hesitant to venture out of the restroom into the darkness of the hallway, where he had heard the sound again. This time, when his watch read quarter to twelve, he heard it moving toward him. His heart sank as he realized that the safety of the bathroom was no longer available; the mysterious machines were closing in on him. He gingerly snuck to the gym locker room, for he loved gym so much, and he hoped to find safety there.

The smell of gym socks and old shoes filled the room and overwhelmed Richard, but the familiar atmosphere of the locker room gave him a false sense of hope. For once he was in the locker room, he sat down on the bench to slow the pace of his beating heart. Once on the bench, Richard looked to the ground with his head between his knee. The bench had a sense of comfort he had not experienced all night. He saw the tracks of a monster machine that he had overlooked, and they looked like monster truck tires all throughout the gym.

Richard was suddenly overtaken by fear that these unseen monsters were closing in on him, and he had nowhere left to go. He sat for what to him felt like thirty minutes but in reality was thirty seconds. Now he could hear the recurring sound of the machines moving, and they were coming for him. They had to be; the sounds wouldn't follow him if they were not. They had found him this time. He thought frantically of where he should run to, and the first place that popped into his head was his very own classroom because it was so familiar to him. Richard ran without looking back.

He got to his room, and out of habit, went straight to his desk and sat down. He had had enough of these stupid monsters. He was stuck in a precarious position with the monsters; he could either try to run to safety again, or he could try to face them. He didn't want to have to spend the night in fear, so he decided to confront them. He jumped out of his seat, walked past his teacher's desk, and froze in his skin. He looked back and his fears were confirmed. He saw his teacher plugged up to a hole in the wall.

Is she recharging? he thought to himself. Richard felt lightning striking him in the heart; he was scared for his life. It was apparent to him that the people he had trusted his education with were really robots.

Then Richard felt the grasp of something strong and metal on his shoulder that gave him a great start. He turned around suddenly, removing the object on his arm, and saw a different robot teacher; he had been caught. In consternation, he backed himself into the corner trying to separate himself from his adversary and conceal his fear, but instead, he surrounded himself even further. He had met his match and had accepted that; he was done fighting for this night.

The robot moved in for the kill when, suddenly, a voice froze the whole room in place. It was the voice of his principal, who he could only hope was human. He had arrived early to get extra work done and saw Richard in trouble.

"Leave him alone, and we will keep your secret from the others," principal Shank shouted seriously. His stare is scary even to a heartless robot. The robot made a mysterious sound of fear and backed away from Richard. Richard immediately extricated himself to the safety of Shank's side. He was safe.

He had become a legend. He had made it through the night with life and limb still intact, but his experiences at that school that night would always haunt him.

a
HUBBARD
Stick Shift Time Machine

If you have ever paid attention in any confined classroom, then you might have learned a thing or two. Such as how Lincoln was assassinated just a week after a different murder attempt was made at Ford's Theater. Or how in old cavemen drawings it looks like a child is bringing them fire. Stuff like that. Well, it wasn't always that way. This is how I, 17 year old Jonas Niccloeson, changed history.

It started out like any other day: with the tantalizing smell of bacon frying on the stove. My mother came into my room, wrenching my curtains open and proceeding to goad me out of my warm, comforting bed. I got up and asked her how she slept, to which she replied that she had slept fine. But I knew that wasn't true because you could see the bags formed under her eyes. She never seemed to get enough sleep in her lonely bed. You might be wondering where my father is, when my mother is right here. Well, my father left before I was born. Mother always told me he left frantically, and when he was informed about me, he claimed I was just a fabrication my mother had made up just to get him to come back. Whenever I asked about it, her eyes would fluctuate from me to the picture she always kept on the mantle, and then she would wince like I had struck her. I looked just like him so I suppose it pained her to look at both of us and be reminded that he wasn't here.

I grabbed my usual clothing: a plain tee-shirt and old, faded jeans. My mother would tell you that my clothing was austere, but don't mind her. A pile of dirty clothes was festering in the corner of my room. I always forgot to put them into the washer, but Mother always forgave my lapse and would wash them for me. I grabbed some bacon from the stove along with a piquant smelling cheese sandwich for lunch. I said goodbye to mother and left to start my walk to school. I took a shortcut through the old car dump but stopped short when amidst the rusting car parts, I saw an old blue classic Chevy. It seemed to be in perfect condition except for some paint chipping, showing its older age. I am a car fanatic, and I couldn't pass up this chance to check out this classic car.

I decided to scope it out and hope my mother wouldn't be too mad if I was late to school. I couldn't find any keys for the car, so using the skill my friend taught me, I hotwired it and drove it down to the old racetrack near the dump. *Good thing my mother has a stick shift because otherwise I wouldn't have a clue how to drive this thing*, I thought. I rolled her up to the faded starting line. I imagined a flag man counting down. 3.....2....1 GO! I slammed my foot on the gas, pushing the car to go as fast as she could. We quickly hit 50 mph...62 mph... 74 mph...78 mph. When we got to 78 mph, the colors outside the windows started running together until it hurt my eyes to look, but I couldn't close them while I was driving. The car came to an abrupt halt, jerking me forward against the seat belt.

Outside the windows was not the old racetrack, but some sort of runway for airplanes. My brain was slowly but surely coming down from the exhilarated feeling of driving that fast. Outside the windshield, a giant crowd was gathered around an old plane. And when I say old, I mean *old*. It was the kind that would only seat one person and find in a museum. When I stepped out of the car, my arm was grabbed by a man dressed in a tweed suit. He was saying something but all I could catch was "landing… Amelia… plane" because of the loud crowd nearby. The man pulled me to the front of the group where a woman was shaking hands and was sporting a pilot's uniform. I was still confused as to what the man had said about someone landing a plane. After a few more minutes of contemplating, something clicked in the back of my mind and everything made sense.

Amelia must be Amelia Earhart, who had just landed her plane. *Holy cow. This cannot be happening. I must be dreaming. There is no way I traveled back in time and am seeing Amelia Earhart*, I thought. I was shaken out of my daze when Amelia came over, shook my hand, and gave me one of her pins she had on her pilot's jacket. When I asked her why she did that, she responded with, "It is so refreshing to see young people interested in something that is happening in the real world."

I am so dreaming right now. But just in case, I better go see if I can get back home, I thought. I bolted to the car and hopped in, quickly starting the engine and driving her down the runway. I was happy that the crowd was paying attention to Amelia and not to me. That would be cause for some interesting news stories. After the blinding colors had faded and my vision had returned, I saw that outside was now a jungle. I was still not home. *Great, where on earth could I be now?* I noticed a giant cave opening to my left with a banging sound coming from it. I went to go see who was in the cave.

As I warily entered the cave, I was overwhelmed by the smell of what could only be described as someone who had never been introduced to showers. I saw a bunch of overly hairy people beating two sticks together. *Cavemen, of course.* They seemed to be trying to do something with long strips of meat. I took the sticks from one of the cavemen, who had dropped it on the ground, and was backed up against one of the walls along with its friends. I built a fire for them, and helped them cook their meat which they quickly devoured. Afterwards, they treated me like I was some sort of god that had given them the key to heaven. When I got back to the car, I, once again, drove it to the 78 mph limit, weaving through the trees, until all I could see was green. The car came to a stop, and through the windshield I could see huge marble columns and buildings.

This must be Ancient Greece. Wow, this looks just like the pictures in my textbook but newer. I didn't think I needed to step out of the car for fear of being impaled by soldiers who were staring at the car and starting to draw their swords. I put the pedal to the metal for hopefully the last time. Now, when the car stopped, I was in Washington, D.C, in front of Ford's Theater. The giant sign displaying the name looked down at me from on top of the building. *While I'm here, I might as well enjoy it.* I went in through a side entrance and took a seat near the back, hoping nobody would notice a strangely dressed teenager. During the performance, a man along with some others went into a special booth decorated with American flags. What caught my attention was the man's tall top hat and dark beard. *There is no way that's President Abraham Lincoln, right? No that is definitely him. So cool, except this must be before he was killed by Booth.* I remember learning about this in school. He died because his guard was at the pub and not his post, allowing Booth easy access to Lincoln.

I went and took the guard's post. Luckily he had left his jacket hanging on the rack, and it had a small hand pistol in the pocket. I had never shot a gun before, but there was a first time for everything. *Maybe a gun and a bow aren't that different, and it won't be that hard. Now I am glad mother made me go to that summer camp, and I learned how to shoot a bow.* When Booth came as expected, I pulled out my gun, as did he. He smirked because I suppose I didn't look very threatening and he could see my hand shaking. Although when he saw that I was serious and would use this gun, his smirk was replaced by a determined look. He got into an offensive position with his gun held up. I raised my gun a little higher and aimed at the bell in the back. When I fired, the sound resonated through the theater and the people, scared by what was happening, were ushered out of the building. Booth did nothing and stood there in the same position, not moving, ready to face me. I shot at Booth's hand holding the gun and twice at his leg in case I missed the first time because of how my hand was trembling out of fear and nervousness combined. I fired at his hand to make him drop his gun and his leg so that he couldn't get away. I then escorted President Lincoln and his guests to the safety of his personal guards. After I made sure everything was okay, I went back to the car.

I started the car again and drove it down the street, and this time I finally got back to the old racetrack. *Fifth time's a charm, I guess.* I continued to school and left the car at the track behind the bleacher. Maybe someone else will find it and have all sorts of adventure. Back at school, the textbook had been modified. It now said the Lincoln was killed a week after his attempted murder at Ford's Theater by an associate of Booth that was later captured and killed. *At least I didn't have too much of an impact, but it was still there. I just hope that car doesn't fall into the wrong hands.*

megan
HULL
The Green Pen
with the Blue Ink

In a small town, just outside of Louisville, stood a middle school. In that school, there was a 7th grade English class with quite a unique teacher who only graded with green pens. Mr. Wilson, a younger man clad in a plaid shirt and khakis, was in the middle of a lesson on gerunds when Tony Matthews, a student in his class, erupted from his chair and yelled, "You're a monstrous man that doesn't deserve to be a teacher here!"

Although it wasn't shown, this comment hurt Mr. Wilson quite a lot. Tony had always been a despicable, mischievous kid, so it wasn't much of a surprise to the class when he wanted to play what he thought was a harmless joke on Mr. Wilson. None of the students knew why Mr. Wilson always used green ink and never any other color, so Tony decided to find out for himself.

While Mr. Wilson was eating lunch, Tony snuck into his room and switched the ink in one of his grading pens from green to blue ink, just to see how he'd react to a new color. What Tony didn't know was that Mr. Wilson was allergic to blue ink, and that's why he only used green. Since Mr. Wilson had so many different grading pens, several days passed with the blue inked pen unnoticed. The day came when he finally picked up the pen to grade a paper while his class was doing a worksheet. He went to click the end of the pen three times like he always did. He clicked it once, and nothing happened. He clicked it twice, and nothing happened. He clicked it one last time, and that's when it happened. The blue ink exploded all over his hands and arms.

Suddenly, he shrieked in absolute terror, knowing the ink on his skin would not be very good for him. The scream alerted the children in the room, and all of their heads simultaneously shot up in his direction to see what the problem was. Almost instantly, the class was overwhelmed in laughter. Mr. Wilson was not very happy with his class, so he quickly told them to get back to work. After that didn't calm them down, he decided to ignore them, knowing soon the ink on his skin would start to take effect. He calmly started taking deep breaths and reached over to grab a few tissues. He tried to get as much ink off as he could, but suddenly, he felt very light-headed and fainted. The laughter abruptly switched to silence when another kid in the class yelled out, "Mr. Wilson is dead!"

All of the children in the class instantly started panicking. One kid ran out of the classroom screaming for help, followed by other screaming children. Teachers and students started flooding the hallways to see what all the commotion was about. The math teacher across the hall came running into the room only to let out a loud cry of her own. She took a minute to collect herself, taking deep breaths, then quickly and calmly pulled out her phone, dialed 911, and explained the emergency to the operator.

In the meantime, other teachers worked together to carry the now unconscious Mr. Wilson down to a couch in the front office to wait for the ambulance to arrive. The school nurse came out to check the rhythm of his pulse and his oxygen level. The ink had caused him to break out in hives all over his body and made it difficult for him to breathe, so the nurse ran to her office to get the emergency oxygen kit and an Epi-Pen. Nobody knew whether to do CPR or just wait. Some said wait, while others said CPR, which caused great dissention among the staff.

The ambulance finally showed up, and the paramedics put Mr. Wilson into the back of the truck and rushed him to the hospital. He came to when they arrived at the hospital, so they took him to the waiting room and waited for an available room. When a room became available, they took him to his room where some nurses helped change him into a hospital gown and got him some medicine to help with the hives. Dr. Biliyar decided to run a head CT followed by an MRI just to make sure he didn't hit his head during the faint. The results came back and showed a mixture of good and bad news. Dr. Biliyar let him rest, so he'd be able to withstand the news when he woke. They put him on several miscellaneous things to help him rest.

Soon after, he gained consciousness and found himself in an empty hospital room. Dr. Biliyar acknowledged him waking up and came in to tell him the CT and MRI results. He said, "You have a small tumor in your brain that will develop into cancer in the near future if it isn't removed. I am able to remove the whole tumor if you want to go through with the surgery. You're very lucky this ink accident happened, or I wouldn't have found the tumor before it developed further."

Mr. Wilson asked if the ink caused the tumor, and Dr. Biliyar assured him that it was not the ink that caused the tumor. Mr. Wilson shed a single tear then thanked the doctor for his magnificent work. He agreed to the surgery, and Dr. Biliyar sent in a nurse to prep him for surgery. When the OR and Mr. Wilson were prepped and ready, they started with the operation.

Dr. Biliyar began by doing a simple procedure called a craniotomy, which gave him access to the location of the tumor. After that, he started to cut out the tumor, being very careful not to hit any major nerves of the brain. He got the full tumor out and finished the surgery by closing up the incisions from the craniotomy. Dr. Biliyar then bandaged Mr. Wilson's head up and sent him to his room. Dr. Biliyar waited patiently for Mr. Wilson to wake up from the anesthesia so he could tell him how the surgery went.

He woke with a massive headache, but Dr. Biliyar said it was normal after brain surgery. Dr. Biliyar sat down in a chair next to Mr. Wilson to tell him the surgery results. He said everything went well, and the surgery was a complete success. He said they were very lucky to have found the tumor at such an early stage. Mr. Wilson thanked him very much, and then Dr. Biliyar excused him to rest.

Tony had heard what happened and felt so terrible that he went out and bought Mr. Wilson a bunch of candy, a get well soon card, and a bouquet of flowers. He took all of this and went to the hospital to see Mr. Wilson. He sat next to Mr. Wilson's bed and waited for him to wake up. Mr. Wilson woke up about an hour later to see Tony had fallen asleep from exhaustion in his chair.

Tony woke up shortly after hearing Mr. Wilson talking to Dr. Biliyar. Dr. Biliyar left, and Tony shut the door behind him. He sat back down, and looked at Mr. Wilson with a very guilty look on his face. Mr. Wilson asked if he was the student who switched the ink. Tony said yes, and that he was so sorry. He said it was only supposed to be a joke, that he never meant to harm him, and asked him to please not be mad at him. Mr. Wilson jumped out of the hospital bed in excitement and said, "If you hadn't switched the ink, then I would've developed cancer!" Mr. Wilson thanked Tony so much for switching it, but told him to never do it again. Tony laughed, said you're welcome, said his goodbyes, and left the hospital with a big smile on his face.

d.j.
HUNTER
Starbucks

Every day I buy an Iced Caramel Macchiato if it's warm outside, and a Caramel Macchiato if it's cold outside. My name is Taylor, and I can assure you the first thing you will ever hear about me from people I know is that I'm a Starbucks fan. Many people have tried to modify my unusual and unhealthy habit, but if I go 24 hours without Starbucks, I go through withdrawal. I become an excruciatingly annoying pain to be around. For example, I start whining about not having my Starbucks, I get angered quickly, and I have a tendency to start throwing the nearest objects at everything and everyone around me.

Since I'm such an avid fan of my daily coffee, I know all of the names of the employees at the Starbucks I go to. I even know the janitor and the proprietor so well, I can tell you they both have a bleak and brusque personality. Since none of the employees were fired or have quit, I was definitely surprised when I walked in one day and saw a new guy working the cash register and coffee machine.

A cursory glance revealed he was clad in a green Starbucks uniform, which meant he was not only new, but also a part-time worker. He had short, brown, curly hair and an athletic build. To me, he was anonymous, but I would endeavor to find out as much about him as I could, because I didn't like not knowing who was fixing my drinks. Ever since I've watched a horror movie where a girl's drink was spiked by a stranger, I refuse to let strangers serve me. Until I learn more about the new cashier, I'll just go to the lady serving at the other register since I know her.

After three daily trips to Starbucks, I have learned a lot about the new cashier, Rick, by observing him. His disposition is sunny, and he evokes laughter and joy from everyone he talks to. When he finds something funny, his laugh pervades the air. I've surmised that he is an affable person that tries not to demean or instill fear into his co-workers or customers. With all these great characteristics, I think I'm starting to have some feelings of affection for him. Also, the coffee he makes look delicious, and I bet it tastes as good as it looks.

It's been four days since Rick has started working at my Starbucks, and I've decided to introduce myself to him. After walking into Starbucks, I head straight for the counter. Instead of ordering a drink, first I say, "Hi Rick, my name is Taylor, and I want an Iced Caramel Macchiato!"

Since he wasn't expecting it, he just stares at me at first, but then he finally pulls up my order and fix my drink. Thankfully, none of the other employees saw me introduce myself to him, since I've never introduced myself to any of the other employees, and I don't want them wondering why I introduced myself to Rick. As I watch Rick use the coffee machine, I notice he tries to subtlety flip the lever on the machine so I get more caramel on my drink. When he hands me my drink, he winks and then says, "Goodbye, Taylor!"

I know it may have been fast, but I just fell in love with Rick. Everything I've seen and heard so far about him tells me he is an amazing person. He fixes great coffee, which is a huge plus. He is also nice to everyone he interacts with, and if someone does something embarrassing, he plays it off like it is no big deal.

The next day I come back and instead of ordering my usual drink, I hand Rick a piece of paper with my phone number on it. As he looks down at the paper, I pronounce, "Rick, I may have just met you, but I'm in love with you with all my heart. I fell in love with you yesterday when you gave me extra caramel. Even though you didn't say it with words, that extra shot of caramel lets me know you love me."

As I finish saying this, I throw myself onto the counter and encompass him with my arms. As soon as I wrap around him, he starts frantically flailing his arms to attempt to escape my grip. Everything turns chaotic, and all that I know is that I'm hugging Rick, and someone is trying to pull me off of him. I even can hear someone yelling for security. Eventually, somebody manages to get me off of Rick, which made me extremely mad, since I was trying to hug the love of my life. I turn around, ready to go off on that person for taking me from my Rick, but then I realize it was a policeman who did it.

The policeman grabs my arm and drags me out of Starbucks. He then proceeds to walk me to my car. When we get to my car, he informs me that Rick is getting a restraining order on me, and once it is in place, I will no longer be allowed in this Starbucks, or within 100 feet of Rick. If I come near Rick or this Starbucks, I will go to jail. How embarrassing, I feel as if I just got roasted. After this day, no matter how much pain I'm in, I refuse to go back to any Starbucks. To solve my withdrawal problems, I've started eating Krispy Kreme donuts every day. Hopefully, I won't get thrown out of Krispy Kreme too.

a
JANESH
The Baseball Incident

Fourteen-year-old twin brothers Ben and Thomas were playing catch in the front yard with a baseball like they do every Saturday. Ben and Thomas' appearances are as different as day and night; where Ben is tall and lanky with blond hair as bright as the sun, Thomas is short and as round as a full moon with Irish red hair. Thomas is the affable kid in school that someone would not go out of their way to talk to, while Ben is one of those popular, spontaneous kids that other kids endeavor to get close to. A characteristic that the twins did share was their psychotic sense of humor.

The weather forecast said that today was supposed to be bleak; however, it was sunny with few clouds in the sky. Since it was a sunny day, the boys decided that they wanted to enjoy it and play catch. When Ben rocketed the baseball towards Thomas, Thomas had to dive to avoid being hit by the ball. Both boys winced when they heard the sound of splintering glass. Thomas tremulously stood up to assess the damage as Ben started cursing like a sailor. Their neighbor Old Lady Carley's car windshield was a spider web of cracks with their baseball sticking out midway through the glass.

Old Lady Carley heard the sound of the impact and came outside. Once she saw her car, she went into a tirade about them damaging her new Toyota and how they were going to regret it.

"Mrs. Carley, I'm so sorry! It was an accident, I swear!" Ben explained.

"Oh, it was an accident, you say?" Old Lady Carley asked with a sardonic smile.

Old Lady Carley, clad in an elaborate blue dress and a baby blue bonnet, put one hand on her hip, the other on her cane. Her waist-length curly grey hair defined her short, petite frame. She gave the twins a look that could kill. The boys stood trembling, and they didn't know what to say. Then, Old Lady Carley started walking towards Ben and Thomas with her cane in her hand to help her hobble over. Ben was terrified, and from Thomas' perspective, it seemed like he was about to be attacked by a dragon. Thomas immediately dropped to his knees and entreated for her mercy, but Old Lady Carley walked straight towards Ben because she did not want to talk to the crying boy on the ground.

"Were you the one who threw the ball?" Old Lady Carley questioned.

"Y-y-yes, ma'am," Ben stuttered.

Old Lady Carley then gave the concise statement, "Then you will pay."

Old Carley then hit Ben in his side with her cane. Ben doubled over clutching his side, but then she hit him in the middle of his back, precisely where he was hit by a football the day before. Excruciating pain pervaded Ben's torso. Thomas tried to break up the fight, but his brother accidentally punched him in the face. Thomas landed on his stomach, and he started to crawl away from the fight. Old Lady Carley then kicked Ben in the stomach with her tan orthopedic shoes, and he fell down on his backside. Old Lady Carley turned around and casually walked away. This will embarrass Ben when he is with his brother or Old Lady Carley for a while. His old neighbor just bruised his stomach and back, and she left the fight without a scratch. Ben has paid his debt.

hudson ray
JONES
The Butler Trials

Jon S. Donsuh represents the mere goals of every early 20th century American man. Proven by the expenditure of money and power that he possesses, however when one gains these desired resources, they desire more and more.

One stunning, bright Sunday morning, Mr. Donsuh came across the urge to hire a butler to help solve his feeling of confinement in his massive four - story, drafty mansion. He already occupies 10 acres of land surrounding his home which is maintained by half a dozen gardeners. However, Mr. Donsuh requires a more classy alternative to the yard workers. One day, he decides to consult Fellis Butler Training school, where he would meet a man in his mid-30's, wearing a goatee named Kaje Winslow, A quite affable lad. Mr. Donsuh would take a great liking to his new-found butler, but to completely trust him, the wealthy gentleman will issue a trial to test his loyalty and trustworthiness.

Mr. Donsuh is, of course, known for his great treasures, which consist of many large collections of jewels and gold. Therefore, it would not be a great surprise as to how he would test Mr. Winslow. In essence, Mr. Donsuh is going to share with his newfound butler that his most valuable treasure is an "ever life" potion. However, It is actually an extremely powerful poison that could slay the largest of horses.

*   *   *

"Mr.Winslow!" Mr. Donsuh explodes toward his butler, located in the far side of the mansion

"Yes, my master?" Mr. Winslow replies in a shaken, fearful voice - scared because if he were to not show up on time, he wasn't sure how Mr. Donsuh may or may not punish him.

"Since we're going to be spending quite a while together, I would like to gift you of the knowledge of my greatest treasure," Mr. Donsuh explains in a tone that even the most foolish of people could tell that he was up to no good.

Mr. Donsuh would explain all about his so called "ever life" potion. The butler obediently listens to his master without a show of much emotion. Nevertheless, The Butler Trials were set into place. The following morning, Mr. Donsuh would rise from a restful slumber from his large and luxurious bed. He began to rise and make his way through the gargantuan mansion towards his precious treasure room. Shaking his head, Mr. Donsuh would find that the seal to the treasure room has been violated. Mr. Donsuh prepares himself for the worst - for all of his precious treasures to be confiscated by his butler. However, to much consternation, Mr. Donsuh would find that not only is the "ever-life" potion untouched, so are the millions of dollars' worth of gold and jewels. Mr. Donsuh slowly backed out of the room and called to his servant.

"Mr. Winslow, come to me now, this instant!"

However, no answer came. Kaje Winslow had disappeared. Mr. Donsuh was alone.

Mr. Donsuh hurriedly rose the following morning to again check on the treasure room. But, to his horror, he would find that his room had also been completely ransacked - fine silk clothes thrown all over the floor, his fine watches and ties all thrown about. But again, none taken.

Mr. Donsuh would find that this man continued to break into his home. Mr. Donsuh came to the conclusion that he would stay up all night to catch the culprit. Four hours and thirty-two minutes after sun down, Mr. Donsuh began to hear a muffled shuffling come into his room. He immediately perked up to catch the culprit who had been coming into his home. He declares in his almost larger-than-life booming voice:

"WHO GOES THERE?!?!"

No reply would come. Mr. Donsuh waits for what felt like a lifetime - which was maybe two minutes. Then again screeches in an even louder more boisterous tone, "SPEAK TO ME, YOU HELLISH BEING!"

The anonymous man waits a short period, as if unsure of what to say. Then whispers, "I can wait, can you?"

Quietness erupts like a bomb throughout the mansion, then again the voice whispers, "I can wait, can you?"

Mr. Donsuh, beginning to feel very mocked declares in a monotonic voice: "Leave my presence, NOW."

No more than a millisecond after Mr. Donsuh the anonymous man declares in a deep, almost satanic voice.

"Go to sleep. You will find your fate to be the one that only the festering excuse for people deserve."

Donsuh jumps up and charges at his adversary, only to find pure air.

"W….What are you?" Mr. Donsuh stammers in a fearful tone. But, no voice replied. The only thing Mr. Donsuh faced was a very familiar vial, filled with a mysterious liquid. It was quite a pretty sight, the way the candle light glistened across the liquid inside. Mr. Donsuh suddenly gained the large urge to drink. Something was pulling him back, but his instincts said to drink. He complies.

Everything began to clear as he drank. He realized that he never was in his bedroom, he had been in the treasure room. However, all of the gold and jewels had been untouched and perfect unlike how he remembered. He immediately began to panic as he sprinted to check on his bedroom to see if it had also never been ransacked.

To much of his horror - he would find that it was in pristine condition. All of his fine clothing and ties in perfect order.

"Mr. Winslow!" Mr. Donsuh attempts to scream in his dying breath..

Immediately, Mr. Donsuh began to hear the footsteps of his butler coming up the stairs. But, it was too late - the wealthy gentleman was already heading to the afterlife.

Mr. Winslow walked into the treasure room to find his master dead, laying in the floor with the "ever life" potion half empty next to him.

Kaje Winslow felt very devastated he knew that his master didn't deserve this fate. Although, he knew that his old master had been treating him as if he were a fool, he still felt a respect for the man that had employed him. But, nonetheless he did try to make me think that he possesses an "ever-life" potion. Winslow began to pick up this phony potion and began to smell it. *Typical* he thought, it smelled strongly of vinegar - *no ever life potion this is.* Evidently, must have been the cause of his master's death. Kaje released a sigh of remorse as he thought: *suicide, such a petty way to go.*

m

KAUFMAN
Funk Engine

It was a new day; a new marching band season. Summer was almost over, and I could not conceal my anticipation, for it was the start of marching band. The lights turned on in my room that I shared with my brothers. We all groaned; we weren't used to waking up early, or at all really due to having no schedule during the summer. Despite our fatigue, we were all wide awake once we remembered what a special day it was. We mentally prepared ourselves for a long day of playing in marching band; it had been so long since we had done so. When I arrived, my eccentric best friend, Dan Smith, was quick to find me, and I was very excited to see him too. I took in the band room; it had been about two months since I had seen the ugly dull paint, the spit-stained floor, and the torturously uncomfortable plastic chairs. Man, did I miss it; it was so beautiful…

Dan Smith quickly pulled me out of my confinement that had been a living hell all summer long, due to the lack of air conditioning and ventilation, and attached my mouth piece. He was incredibly rough about it; it really hurt, or maybe I just needed some oil. Dr. Phil quickly ordered us outside using his megaphone. The band had to rush so we could get in gear and prepare for football games and marching band competitions. We began practicing block marching, the same as every year. However, it seemed Dan Smith was being especially careless for some reason, as he bumped me into one of my brothers. We all fell over, and it made me wince in excruciating pain. Luckily, I only got a small dent and a few scratches on my bell that had "Funk Engine" painted onto it.

Oh, how glorious "Funk Engine" used to be! When Dr. Phil saw it for the first time, he laughed for five minutes straight and gave us an extra water break. Anyways, back to Dan Smith's blunder... I was completely and utterly appalled, as well as bewildered. How had he already managed to screw up like that? Was I just a pawn to him? I meditated upon these thoughts, yet I could find no solution.

The next two weeks of marching band camp passed with few hindrances to the band's progress. The real season was almost here, our first football game was on Friday, and I was fervently wishing it could come sooner. The next couple of days and practices were like a blur, and it was finally time for the game. That's when suddenly, my sloppy player, Dan Smith, dropped me and scratched off some more of the paint that said "Funk Engine." I would subject him to my scathing scorn after this game...

Later, he apologized for dropping me by polishing and painting me. The spray paint that spelled out the words "Funk Engine" looked better than ever now! The band continued practices with Dan Smith being clumsy as ever, beating me up more and more. One day, he managed to drop me with a couple of days before the first competition. Luckily I was in my case, and it was just some lunatic named Carter who hit Dan Smith, but I was still mad. Finally, it was almost time for our first competition. I just loved those. We arrived at around 11:00 A.M, which gave us a few hours to mess around. I just sat in my case while Dan Smith was having fun picking up babes or something like that. Eventually, it was our call time, and Dan Smith and I got ready. When he was coming down the ramp to get off of the band "wagon" he dropped me, and due to being so elevated, it left a massive dent and scraped all of my paint off. I was hideous! Dan Smith couldn't compete, and I was a wreck. Even worse, he didn't even apologize to me! It was a long ride home.

Dr. Phil, one of the band directors, took me to a repair shop the next day to get major remodeling done. I barely felt like myself anymore, and there was another voice in my head that reminded me of the *Duck Hunt* dog. Worst of all, "Funk Engine" was completely cleaned off! By the time I was done being repaired, it was time for the last competition of the season! I was stark-raving mad at Dan Smith! How dare he do this to me! I was going to kill him! I was going to bathe in his blood for what he did to me!

When we got to the competition, I wouldn't cooperate, I wouldn't even let him play me, and I didn't even like this band! That's when tragedy struck. Clumsy, stupid, and completely incompetent Dan Smith had tripped during the competition. This was his worst failure yet: he caused a massive fall for nearly everyone in the band,

and they all fell on me, putting dents all over my bell and making me utterly unplayable.

After that competition, they tried to repair me, but I was never the same. I was never used again, I was never loved, never played, and I was never even looked at. I was shoved into a dark closet, never to see the light of day. My life as the "Funk Engine" was over, and I would probably soon be sent to a scrap yard, if they remembered me at all... I never even got to tell Dan Smith about how I had a crush on him... There was so much I didn't get to do in my short life, and it would all soon be coming to an end. These are my last words... "Push it, push it real good!"

carley
KEOGH
The Trip Gone Wrong

It is the first Monday back from Winter Break, and it was the start of a brand new semester. The students began to scurry around the hallways like ants in an anthill. There was news circulating around Dublin High School that a group of thirteen seniors would be able to embark on a cruise ship for the remainder of their senior year. On board, they would be able to continue their studies and attend classes.

Every senior fervently wanted to experience this once-in-a-lifetime opportunity. The requirements are that: the students must endeavor on their work and studies at all times, as well as have a counselor and teacher recommendation, a notarized waiver of liability to participate, and a medical release form from their primary care physician. Most importantly, they must pass a survival training class, in case anything might happen on the cruise.

It was a week before the seniors would complete the survival training. As the students filed into the school, on the twentieth of January, they noticed a sheet of paper the size of a Jumbotron on the wall. As they walked closer, they realized that it was the sign-up sheet for the survival class. It was a fast, frantic frenzy to be the first one to sign up. The survival training class was going to take place on the thirtieth of January.

On the day of the survival training class, the seniors began to sprint towards the building as they tried to get into the first out of six classes of the day. During the class, they learned how to collect food from nature if they were ever emaciated, how to react if the ship crashed, how to survive in the wild, and how to handle many different crises. By the end of the day, twenty seniors fainted, five seniors needed an ambulance, forty seniors left crying in the middle of the class, and three seniors had a panic attack. Along with these, fifteen seniors had seasickness, a great number suffered from fatigue and nausea, and two experienced dehydration. At the end of the day, there were only thirteen students remaining.

As the trip got closer, those thirteen prepared for their departure. Soon it was the day of the trip, and all thirteen were making their way to Dublin High School. As soon as they arrived at the school, they quickly boarded the dingy bus and drove to the airport, where they were to take the plane to their cruise port. On the way to the airport, construction workers were repairing the hundreds of potholes that had formed over the winter season. Because of this, five of the six lanes were closed. And, all of the traffic was pushed into one lane. As the bus persistently moved along down the single lane like a snail, the students and teachers realized that they were going to be late for their plane. After a grueling drive that seemed to be interminable, they finally made it to the airport, with fifteen minutes left to reach their flight.

After they had passed through security, they only had five minutes to reach their gate. As they tried to find their gate, they all got split up in the gigantic crowds of people. Since they were all in a rush to get to their gate, they never realized that the close-knit group separated into three. One of the three groups accidentally boarded a plane to Tokyo, Japan, another group boarded a plane to Vancouver, Canada, and the third group boarded the right plane to Sydney, Australia.

It took only a mere thirty minutes for everyone to realize that everyone had been separated. However, they knew that they would not be able to find out where everyone else was until after the plane landed. The only problem was that they had no idea where everyone was heading and how long until their plane would land, making it hard to make sure that everyone was safe.

After two days, they were all able to finally call each other to make sure that everyone was okay. When they found out that they were all on different sides of the world, they realized that they would have to cancel the trip and fly back home. Upon their arrival back home, all of the students made sure they took a head count to ensure that everyone was present and did not get separated like they did before. The biggest fear now was how they could explain all that has transpired to the worrying parents.

j.l.
KERERE
The Watch

History was always boring, but today's class was almost painful. I stared out the window as I thought to myself, *Why can't the past be more pleasant? I hate how it's so dark, dreary, and desolate,* when BAM! a textbook dropped onto my desk. Bewildered, I looked up and standing above me was my eccentric teacher, Ms. King.

"Mr. Lane, could you please repeat what I just said?" she asked with a sardonic smile. I contemplated what to say back, but the only thing that came to mind was *I wasn't paying attention* or *George Washington.* After a considerably long amount of time, she merely laughed and walked away. As she started teaching again, my thoughts once again reverberated in my head. I just couldn't help how upset I was with past generations.

The rest of my day wasn't as thrilling. I forgot my headphones in computer class, failed my math test, but won the high jump in the PE so it ended up being a pleasant day. At 2:30, the final bell rang, so I fled the building and started my trek home. About half-way home, I looked to my right and saw an alley. *Huh,* I thought, *I've never seen this before.* I decided to check it out. The only thing within it was a single trashcan. The outside was absolutely disgusting, but when I opened the lid it was spotless, and the only thing inside was a dingy watch. Its beat-up appearance stood out from the futuristic look of the trash-can's interior. "What kind of trash-can is this?" I asked myself as I reached in and picked up the watch; it seemed as if it hadn't been touched in years. The time wasn't even right! Despite its appearance, the watch seemed very old, and I assumed I probably could sell it for a large sum of money, so I decided to bring it home. I stuck the watch into my pocket and returned to my usual path home.

By the time I got there, it was raining cats and dogs. My clothes were soaking wet. I ran upstairs to change before dinner, and I made sure I still had the watch with me. During dinner, my family talked about their days, but I fiddled with the watch. I liked the sound of the clicking it made, so I turned the dial back several times to keep hearing it. All of a sudden, the hands started spinning incredibly fast. I raised my head to ask my Mom for help, but she was nowhere to be found.

None of my family was, or any humans for that matter. Instead of sitting in my kitchen chair, I warily looked around and saw I was now sitting on the roots of a large tree in the middle of a jungle. I heard a screeching noise and saw a shadow fly above my head. I looked up to find the creature, and I recognized it from *Scooby Doo 2: Monsters Unleashed*. It was a giant, flying beast. A pterodactyl! A real one! In the distance, I heard a roar and saw some trees shake; I then realized I had spent too much time in this prehistoric dinosaur land. I assumed the watch brought me here and instead of twisting the dial back, I turned it forward several times until the hands reached about the same speed as before. Almost instantaneously, I was back in my kitchen; it seemed as if no time had passed in my absence.

I asked my parents to be excused, and they both agreed. I bolted up the stairs to my room to think. *I can time travel,* I thought, *I can prevent catastrophes and save lives! Pretty soon people won't even know the name Mount Vesuvius!* I once more began turning the watch's dial back, but not as many times as before. A specific place came to mind, and it was not with dinosaurs.

I was in Ford's Theatre. *Before tonight, nobody even heard about this place,* I thought. I ran to the back door and peered outside to see John Wilkes Booth handing his horse over to a little kid. I immediately locked all nearby doors and brought security guards to see Booth. In Booth's pocket was a gun, and this made the police realize the once well-liked actor's intentions. Twenty minutes later, the Lincolns left the theatre in their carriage and Booth left in handcuffs.

After that, I teleported across the world: I helped fight against the Mexicans at the Alamo, I emptied the gas tanks of the planes in Boston so they wouldn't cause 9/11, and I helped hide Nat Turner so he could lead more revolts against slavery.

When I was finished performing my acts of kindness, I once more turned the dial forward so I could return to my home time. I blinked, opened my eyes, and looked around-- nothing was like home. The world was a moshpit of disaster. Buildings were burning in the background, people were being forced to work, and planes were constantly dropping bombs onto nearby towns. I ran to find insight.

I came across a woman who told me about so many catastrophes that hurt the world. She also said if she found the person who caused them, she would strangle them. My stomach twisted into a knot. I had to make things right. I bet if everything that was altered went back to the way it was, the world would fix itself. I spun the watch's dial many, many times until it was going faster than I had ever seen it before. "Uh oh. What if I go back too far?" Then, in a bright flash, everything went white.

I couldn't see anything, it was so bright. I tried to call for help, but the words couldn't make their way out. The ground below me felt like a cloud, but it slowly began giving away until I was falling through it. I panicked. I was falling through the sky, and I knew soon I would splat. I fell closer to Earth when suddenly, I felt the pressure of the ground smack me. I was out.

BAM! a textbook dropped onto my desk. I looked around and saw Ms. King. "Mr. Lane, this is the second time I've had to ask you today. Please pay attention." The watch had brought me home! I jumped out of my seat in delight. I grabbed Ms. King's hands and danced around. I then ran out of the room cheering; in the distance I heard her yell a threat, but I didn't care. The journey was real, but now I was home! I sprinted out of the building and just before I jumped down the steps, I reached into my pocket, pulled out the watch, and smashed it beneath my foot and threw it into the bushes. "I hope nobody ever finds that stupid thing." I said. I strolled home on my usual route and thankfully, that alley was nowhere to be seen.

j
KIESER
Not a Normal Day at the Trailer Park

It seemed like a normal day in the trailer park for Bobby Dauterive. There was nothing happening in the park, but there never was anything to do anyway. He was sitting silently in his green lawn chair, thinking about how lazy he was most of the time and how his family got mad at him for not getting off his butt. Then at the entrance of the park, Bobby saw a man clad in a black suit walk in. He looked very serious because of his solemn expression. When Bobby noticed the man in black was walking towards him, he began to wonder why. He then wondered if the man walking towards him might be Hank Jackson, his old enemy. They abhorred each other because Hank stole Bobby's valuable first truck. They fought over the truck for a long time, and Bobby finally got it back. He still has it today. Bobby wasn't sure if the man was him because he was so far away.

The mysterious man in black was getting very close to Bobby, and Bobby didn't know what to do. He considered running away as fast as he could, but he realized again that he was lazy and very slow. The man was finally right in front of Bobby and introduced himself as a CIA agent looking for Bobby Dauterive. Bobby quickly responded, telling the man that he was

Bobby because he didn't want to get in trouble with the suspicious man. The agent said he had a mission that needed completion. He explained to Bobby that in this very trailer park, there was a villain named Frank, who has kidnapped a very important person, Richard Miller, and he needs to be freed soon, or the Earth will be a planet of turbulence. The reason it will be is because Richard is part of the UN, and he has to break the tie of the vote for nuclear war. Frank wants the world to be crazy because he abhors many people in many parts of the world, so he is keeping Richard from voting no. The agent explained to Bobby that he was chosen for this mission because he is familiar with the environment in which he will be working. Bobby avidly accepted the offer, so he could be a worldwide hero. The agent said they needed to meet very soon, so they could get started before it was too late.

Bobby woke up the next morning and was ready to leave his trailer in an instant. He was all dressed and clean. The only thing Bobby did was put his special fork in his back pocket for emergency situations. He practices throwing this sharpened fork at a target, so it was a good weapon of choice for him. Bobby got into his truck and got on the road to meet the agent. Bobby finally arrived at the meeting place which was a laundromat, but he waited for hours. He then realized he was barking up the wrong tree; the actual meeting place was across the street at the business building. The reason Bobby finally realized it was because he saw the agent standing in the window. The agent kept looking at his watch and then at the lady next to him. While there, the agent introduced Bobby to his partner, Tammy. She was a little bit on the heavier side and had brown curly hair. She seemed like a nice person, but Bobby couldn't tell for sure. The agent decided this was a mission for Bobby and Tammy, so he didn't come.

Bobby and Tammy prepared to leave by stretching and then hopped into the truck to the trailer park. The truck ride was very concise because of the villain being in Bobby's trailer park. Bobby entered cautiously, while Tammy searched the borders of the park. Tammy heard people yelling at each other in a trailer and immediately called over Bobby. They both surmised that the suspicious trailer belonged to Frank because they saw a silhouette of a person tied up. Frank noticed the duo looking, so he walked outside to demean them and tell them to leave or perish. Bobby and Tammy decided to come back later and check more things out, so they could get more information.

An hour later, when Bobby and Tammy returned to the park, they decided to split up to get more done. Bobby heard Tammy scream for help, so Bobby ran to the location of the voice and saw Tammy being captured by Frank. Not moments later, Bobby was taken by two strong henchman, who were wearing black clothing and black ski masks. They encompassed him with Bobby turning around at just the last second. Bobby was soon brought to Tammy, where they were both tied to the same chair. They were in a dark room where the only light was the faint one right above their heads. Bobby had to think fast to escape and save Richard, who he saw in the other room. All of the sudden, an idea hit him.

Bobby told Tammy to get the fork out of his back pocket. She found his pocket with her hand that was behind her back and gave the fork to Bobby. Bobby then gingerly cut the rope with his fork, that held them tied together, and they extricated themselves from the rope. After that, Bobby threw the fork at the guard, and it stabbed him excruciatingly right in the throat, so the guard hit the ground with a small thump. Bobby opened the door holding Richard inside, but there was no one guarding him. He went up to the tremulous Richard and cut the rope with his fork to release him. The trio silently exited the trailer and entered Bobby's truck. All of a sudden, Frank came running from the back of the house and towards the truck. Bobby then stopped the truck and got out. He tied up Frank and put him in the back of the truck. They then drove back to the meeting place to turn in Frank and Richard.

The agent put Frank in handcuffs and led him to the back of his car. Richard was very thankful for the bravery and courage of Bobby and Tammy. Richard then went on to vote against nuclear war and to keep the world more peaceful. The agent was satisfied with the work of both Bobby and Tammy, so he offered them jobs at the agency. Bobby accepted the offer because he enjoyed helping people stay safe from despicable threats. Tammy unfortunately rebuffed the offer because she liked spending time with her family and didn't want to leave for work every day, not knowing if she will return alive. Bobby went home and enjoyed the thought of having a new job and a new life.

C
KIMMERLING
The Friendly Shark

"Charlie! Get over here right this second!" yelled Mary, Charlie's mother. Her voice was hoarse from the constant screaming at her son. She had a mad gleam in her eyes that made Charlie scared to swim up to her. Mary was fed up with her son. She knew he was dismissive of her constant warnings, but this was going too far.

He should be eating fish, not helping them like he did on a daily basis. Although Mary knew it was inevitable that Charlie would get bored with only assisting fellow sharks and would want to go further with his innate friendliness, she was reluctant to admit it. He was supposed to be a vicious shark, not kind at all, and especially not to fish.

"Mom, I'm sorry. I had seen the little guy struggling to get out of the reef, and I had to help him!" Charlie exclaimed, as he swam up to his mother. She was lingering over a rock that was covered with a thin coat of coralline algae, waiting for her son to catch up to her. Charlie knew that even if he explained himself, his mother would still rage on forever about it; that's just her personality.

"That's not a very suitable excuse, young man. I thought I had told you no matter what, you don't help any fish in the ocean! Do you understand me? I barely tolerate you helping our own kind, let alone the ones we feast upon for dinner. I'm sorry, but it just causes way too much speculation, and not only is it atrocious, but it looks bad on our whole species," Mary explained, looking expectantly at her son as she continued, "I mean, if you are going to be amiable, at least be discreet about it. If I descry that you have been aiding any breed that is not our own, I will send you to the outskirts of the most remote island I know, and you will have the privilege of spending the rest of your life there! Do you understand the words that I am saying?" Not waiting for her son's response, Mary swam away, done with her youngest son's antics.

"Okay mom, I understand," said Charlie dejectedly. Even though Mary had left, he knew that his mother was never going to forgive him for his wrongdoings. She was the type of person that held a grudge for a long time and took forever to forgive someone. Wanting to be alone, Charlie started to swim towards his treasured coral reef, one that he had been going to habitually since he was seven and had discovered it. He always went there when he was upset and wanted to alienate himself from the world. As he was swimming, he saw a brief coruscation of an old, brown, dingy cloth being dragged along in his peripheral vision. He wasn't sure what exactly was pulling the cloth, but he knew that it was small and had neon viridescent scales covering the entirety of its body.

After staring after it for a while, he surmised that it was actually a fish that was toting the calico along.

Charlie had resolved that he was going to find out the reason that the tiny fish was carrying a cloth around in his mouth, not just because he was curious, but because he knew that it would make his mom angry and that is exactly what he wanted. He started to swim after it when there suddenly was a grey blob swimming around him, and he realised it was his brother.

"Hey Charlie, what are you doing all the way out here? Going to help some poor fish?" Charlie's brother, Frederick, taunted.

"None of your business, Fred. Don't you have something better to do than bug me?" Charlie replied, not waiting to hear his brother's response as he swam away. His oldest brother had always been mean to Charlie, and Charlie had decided about two years ago to be as vague and introverted as he could be when he was around Frederick. Shaking off his brother's comment he started to swim towards the fish once again.

He caught up with the small fish and was about to stop and introduce himself, his mother's previous warnings forgotten, when he felt a shift in the water around him. He felt the water start spinning around him, and he realised he got caught in a whirlpool.

He was in the whirlpool for about five minutes when it died down, and he swam away. He picked up the trail of the fish and started his chase again. After about ten minutes, he saw James the giant squid and the fish arguing.

"Hey, leave him alone!" Charlie yelled at the giant squid, knowing him to be a jerk to everyone.

"Well, well, well, look who it is. Look, Gillbert, it's the guppy loving nurse shark, Charlie," said James to Gillbert, who was the fish who Charlie had been chasing.

Since Charlie could tell that James was only going to be mean and taunt them both, he decided to get this over with and attack him, even though Charlie's fighting skills weren't the best. James would be a difficult adversary to beat. He charged the squid and tried to bite him, but James hit his stomach, and Charlie fell to the ocean ground barely moving, but enough for him to get air. Charlie usually wouldn't use violence, but this called for it, as he was strangely attached to the small fish. He had grown on him, and Charlie wasn't used to feeling this way towards someone because most people think of him as weird and crazy for being nice. Because of the dislike towards him, Charlie had no friends and even though he tried to make them, everyone had mutually agreed to

Gillbert, the tiny fish that Charlie had chased all day, picked up a loose piece of coral that was on the ground and charged James. Gillbert hit him in the eye, knocking James out from the pain of getting stabbed in the eye. He swam over to Charlie, who was still in agony, although not as bad as before. Gillbert stayed next to Charlie until he could swim again and they decided to become friends, Charlie not caring about what his mother said.

KLEIN
Eight and Elbowless

Joe was an eight year old boy who lived a simple life with his two parents. Every night he would do his homework, eat dinner, shower, have some free time, and then go to bed around 9:00 pm. Every week day morning, he would wake up at 7:00 am to get ready for school, and his parents would leave for work. Joe was just your average kid. One Monday morning, Joe's alarm clock went off at 7:00 am as usual. As he tried rolling his way over his left arm to stop the annoying sound of his alarm clock, he noticed that his arms were unusually stiff. He began to try and move around a bit to loosen up, and suddenly his normal, squinty-eyed morning face turned gruesome as he slowly began to realize that he had no elbows.

"Ahhhhh! Where are my elbows?" Joe exclaimed frantically.

He became tremulous at the bizarre situation he was in. He carefully began to evaluate his elbowless arms, which were as hard and straight as pegs, being cautious that he didn't make matters worse. Joe was so appalled by the situation that he became utterly still and contemplated what to do next. After a few moments, he took a deep breath, rolled out of the bed and warily made his way to the hall bathroom to take a look at himself. Sure enough, the unusual scenario was reality.

"How did this even happen? Was mom right about the bad things that could happen to you if you ate chocolate after 8:00 pm?" Joe thought to himself while giving a bewildered look to himself the mirror. He had snuck into the kitchen late last night around 9:00 pm to get some chocolate after his parents were in bed, but quickly erased his mom's ridiculous myth from his mind.

Luckily, he hadn't had to open any doors yet that morning, since he slept with his bedroom door open and left the hall bathroom door slightly ajar. He hastened to the kitchen to see if his mom may have still been home, as she sometimes was at that time, which was now 7:17 am. Unfortunately, she was gone. He decided to call his parents and tell them about his eccentric condition. As he awkwardly walked stiff armed to the kitchen phone, he remembered that he couldn't grab the telephone that was placed high on the shelf above the cabinets. After multiple times trying to reach the phone, he finally gave up. As he was walking toward his living room, he saw the time: 7:30 am. He had to catch the bus at 7:45 am for school and he hadn't even started to get ready. Without elbows, he was much slower at getting ready than normal.

Joe had always been on top of his perfect attendance for school since kindergarten, and he wasn't about to ruin it all. He knew that his arms, lacking elbows, would be noticeable. Even though it was 87 degrees Fahrenheit outside, he planned to wear a long sleeve shirt to help him not be so distinct from the rest of his classmates. He soon realized how hard it was to change your clothes when you couldn't bend your arms, but it was vital that no one at school knew that there was something wrong with him or he would get teased by his classmates. Joe ended up slipping on a jacket as quickly as he possible could, slithering one arm in, then leaving his Mario Kart pajama pants on, and putting on a pair of worn out tennis shoes. The clock now said 7:44 am and without even thinking about breakfast, he flung his arms to push the button to go out the garage door and began to run down his long driveway to catch the bus.

All he could think of is that no one would notice his appearance and that everything would hopefully be fine, but he was still apprehensive. As he saw the bus come to a stop at the end of his driveway, everything in front of him began to fade. Soon enough, he was back in his bedroom again, hearing the repeated beeping sound of his alarm clock, and he was joyful to realize that it was all just a dream.

"Boy am I glad that I have elbows again! I thought I was going to have an ulcer!" Joe was so excited to see and feel that he had his elbows back again.

As he was about to hop out of bed to begin his usual morning routine, he looked down at his feet and saw that he only had 3 toes on each foot.

"Nooo! Not this again!"

Poor Joe just couldn't get a break.

LAMB
Meeting Mr. Wilson

I thanked the affable lady as she handed me the thing I had been looking forward to see all day: the schedule for my eighth grade year. Of course I was excited, but I was also more nervous than anything. I've been told some things about the teachers. I heard that a few were irascible, and that their classes seemed to last an interminable period of time. However, I had also heard that some were funny, interesting, and casual. I didn't really have a specific teacher in mind that I wanted to get; however, there was one teacher that I was a little scared to have. I had heard that he was funny, but extremely terrifying when angry. Remarkably, the one teacher that I was nervous to get, turned out to be one of the best teachers I've ever met. His name was Mr. Wilson.

First and second block went by considerably fast. Both blocks consisted of getting to know all of the new students and the teacher. I was happy with the overall classes. I had a lot of friends in them, and the teachers seemed calm. After the bell rang to end second period, I began my journey to English class. I walked to Mr. Wilson's class with two of my friends, constantly looking down at my schedule to see the room number, and we all were talking about what we thought the class would be like.

"I've heard he's funny. I hope it's true," one girl said.

"I did too, but I also heard he gives a lot of work," I sighed. They agreed, and we continued walking. As we turned the corner and began pushing through the turbulent eighth grade hallway, we saw him standing outside of his doorway. He looked very intimidating with his straight-face and high stance, so we all exchanged tremulous glances. We continued walking and tried to emulate a completely normal, not nervous student.

"Hi," he said casually as we approached the door.

"Hello," we all mumbled nervously. I saw a smile creep on to his lips, so I guess he enjoyed the fact that we were nervous. Yeah, that didn't help. I walked in to see a lot of my friends in the classroom. I quickly moved to find a good seat near them, and I found one right in the front row. I tried my best to neglect the bad thoughts about him yelling at us, obscure all of my worries about hours of homework, and engaged myself in a conversation. Then I heard a bell ring, a door close, and a man whistling to the tune of *Star Wars*.

All of the heads turned towards the door, and the whistling stopped. We watched him as he walked towards the front and center of the room slowly, his feet walking loudly. Once he reached the front of the room, he stood there as we all stared. He smiled awkwardly, making us all laugh. Mr. Wilson began talking about himself: what he liked, and what he didn't like. For example, he has a strong love for hot chicken, but he hates us. I never knew that a person could love spicy chicken so much until that day! Laughter pervaded the room as he made weird, yet funny, jokes about how much he hated the students.

I think I'm going to like this class, I thought.

"Okay, fun time is over. Let's talk about the work. There will be essays due Wednesdays and Fridays, vocab due Monday, two books a month..." Mr. Wilson said and the list went on and on. This amount of work was completely spontaneous and new to the students. I looked around me to see people's eyes widen as they bit their nails or pencil. I mean, I barely have enough time to myself now between volleyball and spending time with friends and family, how will I get by with so much work? My own thoughts began to stress me out as he kept discussing work, when things were due, future projects, and the guidelines for the class.

"Any questions?" he finished.

"N-No," we all nervously stuttered as he giggled.

"Okay, now, we're going to talk about seating arrangements tomorrow, but just as a heads up, I'm going to be calling you guys by your last names," he said.

Oh great, my last name is Lamb, I thought to myself, subtlety rolling my eyes. He joked around some more and showed his funny and awkward side, which got rid of the tension in the room. I looked at the clock, and it seemed that the bell was going to ring soon. I packed my things and waited patiently for the bell to ring as he answered questions. Finally, the bell rang, interrupting him. He groaned and said goodbye, and we all scurried out of the room as fast as we could! We weren't scared, but we were all anxious to get out of this class and continue on with the day. I ended up enjoying myself for the next couple of days. I couldn't be happier with the class, and after about a week of the class, I knew it'd end up being my favorite!

m

LANE
Birthday Gone Wrong

The streets were lonely, and there were no sounds besides my car engine running. As I got closer to the club, the buildings began to look old and run down. I saw the billboard that read "Dance all night," and knew I had finally made it to the random dance club. I parked my car, walked up to the brick building, and went straight for the door. After minutes of struggling to get the door open, I finally was able to get inside only to see the lights were off. I was so bewildered. How could my friends lead me to a closed club with a banged-up door for my twenty first birthday? Right when I was about to walk out to text my friend, Suzy, who gave me the address, my ears were filled with a sudden "Surprise!"

I was left appalled and thinking that I was on a prank show or something. When the lights were turned on, I saw all these familiar faces which left my veins pulsing with exhilaration. There were decorations, confetti, and lots of people. I never thought this huge crowd would come and celebrate my birthday. I shed my casual and bleak jacket that I wore because it was cold outside and jumped right into socializing and dancing.

Everything was great! I met new people and danced until my body felt fatigued. Since that was probably from dehydration, I headed over to the bar to get some water. The bartender handed me my drink, and I headed right back to the center of attention. While I was making my way over to Suzy, some guy spilled his beverage all over the front of my outfit, which left it sodden. I was so angry, but I knew he didn't intend to spill his drink on me. So I kindly accepted his apology and told Suzy I was going to the bathroom to clean up. Once I dried off, I decided to take a walk to clear my mind.

I kept walking in and out of random alleys and streets just to realize I had lost track of where I was walking and somehow alienated myself in a desolated area. Just like all the other buildings in that section, everything was made from old brick. This made the fact that I was lost even more stressful. I was trying really hard to get back, but ended up getting way too frustrated because I had no idea where I was. After a few minutes of mentally scolding myself and trying to calm down, I finally decided to make a rational decision and call my friend Suzy. However, luck was not on my side, so naturally she didn't even answer. And to make it worse, I had two percent of battery left since I forgot to charge my phone earlier. I put my phone back in my purse and started to walk in the opposite way because I was determined to get back to my party.

While trying to retrace my steps, I saw the club's billboard in the distance. It read the same thing, "Dance all night." But there was conflict, because I saw two ways. It was either walk three blocks or cut that time in half and walk the alley. The safest decision was clear, but I already missed like thirty minutes of my birthday party and that was just too much precious time. So to the alley I went with great ambitions, which slowly started to turn into regret. The alley was long, narrow and was made up of brick building remnants left from unfinished construction work. I almost made it out, but a foul smell grabbed my nose, forcing my eyes to meet the ones of an eccentric-looking person. He was clad in dingy clothes that were brown from lack of cleanliness.

Being me, I somehow couldn't get my legs to listen to the vital signals that my brain was sending to them to move. I winced when he grabbed my arm from sheer fear and pain. All that was going through my head was, *I was going to die*. But I needed to stay strong. I slapped him with my free hand, but he had the nerve to grab it and throw me into the brick wall, which ended up with me on the ground. My head felt woozy, and my eyes were a little cloudy after taking in the impact from the throw. I tried to scream, but it was no use because a dirty hand had been clasped over my mouth. I tried to bite his hand, but he only pushed down harder. I wanted to give up, but I just couldn't. My last resort was to look for something hard. While he was going through my purse, I felt around the ground for anything and found a stray brick. When he turned around, I hit him in the head as hard as possible.

His body went stiff. I thought he was dead, but just to confirm it, I checked his pulse. It was faint but still there which meant he was still alive. After collecting my purse and using some hand sanitizer from it, I decided to use my two percent to call the police and report a theft so he would at least get put in jail. I wanted nothing to do with it so I had left the address to the police and walked back to the club.

When I finally made it back, the club had the same party atmosphere as it had when I left. I talked to Suzy about what happened, and she agreed to keep it a secret, since I practically killed him and wanted nothing to do with it. I ate cake, danced, and opened up some presents. I still kept on feeling a little uneasy about the whole incident and knew that I was going to have to deal with it sooner or later, so I decided to let go for the remainder of the night. I let myself feel like a scarf floating in the wind, being taken wherever. Never looking back.

9
LAYHEW
Lonely Island

I awoke from my sodden, desolate bed of grass after an interminable night filled with rain showers and mosquito bites. I sat up in an erect position to observe my surroundings for anything that could hold a potential threat. It had been three months since the ship sank, and I sat on this island with no one to speak to and nothing to do. Only a few remnants of the shipwreck remained: a matchbox, a few canned goods, a flare gun with two flares, and a useless old volleyball. I have survived by building a small shelter from a few tree limbs and using my skills I learned as a young boy to catch small fish with a spear I made from a stick and a sharp stone.

I arose from my makeshift bed, not remembering the wound I had on my leg from falling out of a tree a few days ago where I was trying to find any signs of rescuers from the precarious position. I fell in agony as pain surged through my body, sending me to the ground, hitting a tree limb on the way down, leaving small abrasions on my arm. It was then that I felt the coldness pervade my body because of my wet and dingy clothes. I carefully got up and limped over to my fire pit to retrieve a match to light a small fire to warm me. As I grabbed the small wooden piece, I noticed a bottle on the shore.

I wobbled over to see that it was an empty bottle of water. Closer investigation led me to deduce that it was fairly new. I didn't know if it was an indication of a nearby ship, or if it was merely a coincidence. I limped away from the bottle to go to the pathway I had laboriously carved from the tall grass with a hatchet I made from a dull, blunt stone. The path led to the singular fresh water source on the bleak island. I put the empty can of beans into the water and drank the dirty, murky water. I looked around for any small rodents I could catch, but I saw nothing. I then focused my attention on the gleaming sun which reassured me that people haven't given up hope for me. I slowly made my way back to my small, quaint camp. As I walked, I kicked and dragged the volleyball with me to pass the time it took to get back.

When I returned to the camp, I fell due to exhaustion. My leg and arm were still throbbing in pain. On top of my aches, I then felt my stomach grumble violently. I grunted in agony as I got up and crawled over to my stockpile of three old fish. They may have started rotting, but I couldn't care less. I grabbed one as I looked out at sea to watch the sunset which made a beautiful scene, ironically. I prepared the fish on the fire I had sparked with one of the few remaining matches. After waiting impatiently for the fish to cook, I took it out and ate everything except the bones and eyes.

Night had come quickly. I looked up at the moon and began drifting off to sleep. A howling horn woke me instantly. I looked across the ocean to see a dim light. I sprang up, ignoring my pain, and rushed to get my flare gun, I picked it up and pulled the trigger. Nothing happened, so I pulled it again and the flare shot right into the water. My incompetence had cost me a flare and maybe my only chance of survival. I knew I had a single remaining flare and had to make it count. I loaded it, pointed up, and shot. After a few seconds that felt like hours, the ship blew its horn again. I squinted and could make out a silhouette of a helicopter getting ready to take off. I cheered in glee as it took off. I was going home.

katie
LEE

The birds fluttered from tree to tree. It was finally spring, and the plants had sprung alive, clothed in color. Spring didn't just mean new colors and aggravating allergies, but to sixteen-year-old Blair, it meant Easter. Easter was a time of family, food, friends, God, and Easter egg hunts. Every year, there is a county-wide Easter egg hunt, and every year the prize gets bigger and better. For example, last year's reward was a car, and the year before that, a pet monkey! Blair has never won, but she has always wanted to. In five minutes, the news will announce the prize for this year's hunt. Blair hoped it would be something spectacular like a shopping spree to a store of her choice or something very expensive. She stared at the television screen with anticipation.

The professional looking news anchor, who wore lots of makeup, spoke with great eloquence as she announced the prize for this year's Easter egg hunt will be worth one million dollars! Blair stood still at the thought of a remarkable trip to Paris, endless pairs of shoes, and a whole new wardrobe; all the things she wished to do with one million dollars. She could not wait for the hunt. Blair prepared by picking out the perfect outfit, so when her picture is in the paper for winning, she can look her best.

After eight restful hours of sleep, Blair was at the event, determined to win. Crowds of people swarmed everywhere like bees near a hive. Blair stood atop the hill near the entrance and overlooked the field in which what seemed like thousands of eggs of every shape, size, and color sat behind one huge statue of a golden egg. A look of utter amazement spread across Blair's face as she admired the huge statue. The volunteer workers lined the people of all ages, shapes, and sizes on the sodden grass, for the hunt was about to commence.

The horn sounded, and everyone sprinted toward the field and the egg they hoped would give them a million dollars. It was complete chaos. Blair made it to the statue, and only one small blue egg lay on the ground. She made her way over to it and was pushed down by a man who was much bigger than her. Appalled at the treatment she had received, she gathered herself together and stood up. Hesitant to try and go on, Blair just stood there. There wasn't an egg near her, and heaps of people were fighting over the eggs left. Blair realized with no egg, she would have no chance of winning. She gave up and decided to take a seat on a conveniently located chair at the base of the statue until the horn would sound and announce the winner.

A single, rather large egg lay on the chair Blair intended to sit on. Hoping to get at least one piece of candy out of the day, Blair opened it to see what it concealed. It was a remote with one button. With a bewildered expression, she hit the button and jelly beans rained down from the giant egg statue. Blair was shocked and didn't move for a long moment. She then realized the remote had opened the egg statue and sent this rainstorm of jelly beans. Everyone paused and stared. It was dead silent. Over the loudspeaker, a voice boomed that the grand prize egg had been found.

It took Blair around twenty seconds to realize the voice over the loudspeaker was talking about her. She was thrilled she had won, but slightly disappointed the reward was one million dollars' worth of jelly beans instead of the cash prize she hoped for. One million jelly beans cannot buy her a trip to Paris like the money could. But Blair decided to look at the winning in a positive way. So with everyone watching her, she took a hand full of jelly beans and shouted "Does anybody want some candy?" Everyone cheered and the jelly beans were shared. To say the least, there were more than enough to go around.

j. ryan
LEVINE

I'm laying down in my bed which is turbulent because of my nightmares. My room is clad in a deep shade of blue. I have a sardonic smile on my face because of the horror movie playing from my television. On my floor, there is an anthology of the horror stories that I have collected over the years. My name is Victor Green, but my pseudonym is Leonid Khrushchev.

I have to use that fake name because I'm an escaped mental hospital patient, so in other words... I'm a lunatic. My stomach growls like a lion, so I leave my disgusting room to go to the mall's food court for a meal. Also, I need another victim. I need some fun in my life. I lean against the railing with a *McDonalds* hamburger that I just bought in my hand. There is a small crowd in the food court, so I try to find a loner. A few moments later, I spot one who had just gotten his soup from the Chinese fast food place that people seldom went to. I rush down the stairs to intercept him. I decrease my rhythm of two steps at a time down to one. I get off the stairs at the bottom and make my way to my target, a man who looked about five foot eight. I bump into him as hard, but also as subtly, as I can. Since I spilled his soup on the floor during the bump, I asked if I could give him the money for it or buy him another one. It was a habit of mine, but he turned me down.

I went to the bathroom and changed my clothing, changing into more casual clothes. I came out wearing khaki shorts and a tee shirt. I left the bathroom, now empty, for I was the only one inside and I threw out the rest of my hamburger, which I had been neglecting. I saw the man leaving the mall I began to follow at a distance. The man I was following was a sitting duck, and I was the hunter trying to kill him...

In the center of the large town I was in, there were several large buildings. My target was entering a black building that was about two-hundred feet tall. I enter approximately 10 minutes after he does. I enter the building, and I get the room number by pretending to be the man's brother. I walk up the stairs to his room and quietly turn the door knob. It was unlocked. I opened the door slowly, careful not to make a sound. I creep up behind him and grip his throat with my long slender fingers.

A few minutes later I check his pulse to corroborate that the man was dead. I left the hotel room and made my way downstairs. The women at the counter greeted me and we talked for a while until suddenly two policemen rushed in a cuffed my red, bloody hands.

C
LOPER

As I awoke to the sound of my alarm, I looked to the side of my bed to see my alarm clock flashing 7:50 am. I had to get to school in ten minutes! I jumped out of my tall bed, so high I hit my head on the ceiling. If I was late to school one more time, I would get ISS. Since that would mean I get my third ISS, which leads to OSS for two weeks. I rushed to my closet and threw on my clothes as fast as I could. I ran out to the car that was sitting in the driveway. I hopped in my car and tried to start it, but nothing happened when I turned the key. I gave the car a cursory review and could not figure out why it would not start. I ran back into the house and yelled to my dad "I'm taking your car!" I was out the door before he could answer.

It was already 7:59, as I raced to school. I only had one minute to get into my classroom before the bell. Of course with my luck, I also forgot all my school supplies at home, but I had not time to retrieve them. All I had on my mind was getting to school. As I turned onto Lake St., which is about a block away from my school, the car started to make an erratic noise, and I knew something was amiss. All of a sudden, the car stopped, my heart dropped, and I knew I was not going to get there in time.

I called my dad to come pick me up in my mom's car, and we took off for school. Luckily for me, my dad was already on his way to work so I only waited for thirty seconds. When I got in the car, I told him I had no time for questions and had to get to school fast. He pulled into a parking spot, and I leapt out of my dad's car. I ran as fast as a cheetah into school. It was too late when I arrived, class had already begun, and I knew I was in big trouble. I casually walked into the classroom, hoping the teacher would overlook me, but I heard Mr. Sanderson say "Well, it's nice to see you, Mr. Heart, but it looks like you're late, and you know what that means."

It means another ISS, in school suspension, which is my third of the year. I got my first by gluing Mrs. Born to her seat on the third day of school. Mrs. Born never seemed to get past the fact I did that to her. Mr. Sanderson told me to go down to the office and wait for my parents. The school was calling my parents and sending me home for two weeks. Now it might sound great not having school for two weeks and no homework, but it is going to be the complete opposite of that.

As I walked into my house, I glanced back to see my last gleam of sunlight, because I will be grounded forever. I hesitantly walked into the front door of my house to see my mom and dad sitting in the living room. I could see the disappointment in their eyes. As I walked in, they summoned me to come sit down. When I sat down, they looked at me and my father said, "You have some major explaining to do young man."

I sat there for a good hour as my mom went on a tirade about getting in trouble at school. I tried to say it was not my fault. I explained how my car was messed up, and I wouldn't have got in trouble if I had a brand new car. Of course they did not believe me. They finally decided on my punishment: they said I would be grounded for 4 months. They were also taking my phone away for 4 months, and I was appalled it was that long. They proposed a year if I kept arguing.

So as it might seem getting OSS or grounded is fun because you do not have school; it's not, trust me. Finally, I returned to school two weeks later to see that I was failing every class. My mom is not finding out about that or my four months will turn into four years.

octavia n.
MARTIN
Powers

It was a bleak day in the town of Seattle, Washington. Robbie Peterson, who was just waking up, felt as if there was something different about the day, though. Even though he felt that way, he still went through his methodical routine in the morning. His daily schedule consisted of him having to rub his weary eyes, taking a scorching shower, and reluctantly getting dressed, but today he felt the exact opposite. He wanted to get up and take his shower.

Soon after, Robbie got out of the shower, he went to go grab his clothes off of the dresser, but he was appalled at what happened next. His clothes started floating in the air, and they began to move towards him! It was as if he had summoned the clothes. He was bewildered at what had just happened. Robbie didn't know what to think. He tried to reassure himself that it was just another one of his brothers pranks, like the time his brother put goo all over his bed. When Robbie went to sleep he was covered all in it. So Rob told himself it was nothing and snatched his clothes from the air. Then he put them on and went downstairs to eat breakfast.

Right after he got done with breakfast, he hurried to get on the bus. As he got on the bus, he kept dropping his books that were in his hand. As soon as he went to pick it up, they started floating to him like they were a hoverboard. He knew this couldn't be one of his brothers pranks because his brother could never fabricate a prank like this one.. There had to be something wrong!

He sat down in his seat and tried to overlook what happened; however, Rob had a remarkable amount of questions in his mind such as why had this happened to him, or what would occur next if he didn't figure out what was going on. Eventually, he decided not to overlook the situation that was taking place and find the truth about what was going on.

Robbie was so glad he decided to find out what happening to him because he was having so much fun with what he soon found out was telekinesis! He could do so much with his powers like get a pencil on the floor without moving an inch, or he was allowed to get his stuff from his locker without having to go to it. Although he thought his powers were amazing, and everyone would think they were awesome, he knew he couldn't show anybody. He decided to try and use his powers with no one looking. Robbie also decided he didn't want to tell his parents either. So he went on to some more experimenting with his powers, but something strange started happening to him and his powers. He couldn't control them. Whenever he wanted the object to go left, it went right. Also, stuff that he didn't want coming to him still did. He knew he had to do what he didn't want to do, Robbie had to tell his parents.

After the day ended, Robbie got on the bus, went home, and started talking to his parents. They asked Rob the usual questions: how was your day? What did you do? He cut to the chase and told his parents what he found out that day. To his shock, his parents weren't surprised! In fact, they were happy. They told him they knew this day would come, and they were glad that he told them because they had powers too. Now they could give him guidance for his powers. They told he had to use his powers responsibly, or they will act up. He could not go around and recklessly use them. He was glad he told his parents because now he could control his powers without being worried.

e
McDANIEL

Finally, there would be a day with no rain! Blair and her dad had been in Seaside, Florida for a week now, and most of their plans had been canceled as it had rained six of the seven days. Blair's dad, Bill, finally found a day on the forecast that looked nice. Bill had told Blair the night before that he was going to take her scuba diving the next day, and she was ecstatic! Blair went to bed earlier than she usually did on vacation, since she had a big day ahead of her; however, she couldn't sleep so she decided to look up some information on scuba diving, since it would be her first time. Blair pulled up a few different official scuba diving websites and was shocked to see that there were some bad things that had happened while scuba diving, such as running out of oxygen while underwater and shark attacks. But this didn't worry her because she knew she would be safe. A few minutes later, Blair decided she would hit the hay for the night.

It was seven o'clock in the morning, and the day of scuba diving had begun, so Blair jumped out of bed. She could hardly stand her excitement as she put on her favorite bikini. She rushed up the stairs of her family's vacation house to get her dad up out of bed, but to her surprise, he was already in the kitchen getting breakfast ready. On a normal day, Blair had to drag her dad out of bed, but not today: he was too excited. Blair and her father finished breakfast and jumped into the car.

The whole way to the facility they talked about what they thought it would be like. They both thought it would be a nice relaxing day looking at all the interesting things in the ocean. They finally arrived at their destination. Blair got inside, and she met her instructor, PJ, who excitedly said, "Hi, I'm PJ, and I'll be helping you through the adventure of scuba diving." Blair was so excited after she put on her wetsuit, but she remembered the websites she had viewed and the nerves started to settle in her stomach

PJ gave Blair's father their flippers, oxygen tanks, masks, and directions to the boat dock. Bill and Blair jumped in the car and drove to the dock. Now, she really started to get nervous. She hopped onto the little pontoon boat behind PJ, being careful not to trip on her flippers. Her body felt confined in her wetsuit, like she was a butterfly in a cocoon. As soon as the boat started going towards the spot they would descend from, Blair started to fluctuate between whether she should go or not. But her dad convinced her it wasn't going to be scary, and that it would be fun; however, Blair couldn't help but think about the terrifying things she had seen on the internet the night before.

It was finally time to jump out into the ocean. PJ went first so he could assist Bill and Blair, then Bill jumped, and it was now Blair's turn to go. She fervently wanted to see everything in the ocean, so she jumped. The three of them went underwater to test out the masks and then started to descend. On the way down, Blair saw some colorful fish, extraordinary reefs, and some distinct plants, and she loved every second of it! Blair looked to the top of the water and saw a gleam of sunlight shining down onto her wetsuit. Then she looked to her left and saw a quick glance of a "dolphin," or that's what she thought. Blair then realized that it wasn't a dolphin she was trying to touch, because dolphins don't have sharp teeth like that: it was a shark.

She tried to swim away, but it was too late. The shark's mouth opened wide and snapped down on Blair's left hand. After the shark bit Blair, it quickly swam away. PJ frantically signaled Bill, so they could help Blair. She tried to scream, as she felt the agony in her hand. Blair went into shock because of the attack. Her dad was scared it would be a precarious situation, as he and PJ rushed Blair to the shore that was forty feet away. It was obvious that Blair was in pain, so PJ called 911 as soon as he could stand up in the cold ocean water. As they waited for the ambulance, both Bill and PJ tried to calm Blair down.

The ambulance got to the shore about fifteen minutes later, and Blair was rushed inside. The paramedics put the oxygen mask on her as fast as possible. She had passed out seconds before this because of all the blood she had seen coming off her what used to be her hand. Bill thought to himself, *I am so crazy for letting my daughter do this: it's all my fault.* The paramedics looked at Blair's red arm from all the blood and told her father and

PJ that her left hand was gone but that was all they could see just from their cursory evaluation.

When the ambulance pulled up to the hospital, the paramedics pulled the stretcher out and ran inside. Her father and PJ were right behind them every step. When Blair was taken into the emergency room, her father tried to follow, but they told him he must wait in the family room. He walked into the bleak room, thinking constantly about his daughter and hoping he wouldn't lose her.

After about a million hours, Blair's dad was finally allowed to see his daughter again. He contemplated what he should say but decided to reassure her that everything was going to be okay, and that he was so sorry. Blair woke up after about four hours, and the first thing she said was that scuba diving was so much fun. Her dad thought she was crazy based on what had happened, but he just let it go because she was on a bunch of medications. Bill let his daughter rest, and he went to go talk to the doctors. They said, "Blair lost a considerable amount of blood and her left hand, but other than that she is going to be perfectly fine." Her dad couldn't believe that she lost a hand, but he couldn't be happier that Blair was going to be okay.

Blair had a few weeks of recovery and physical therapy since she had one less hand. She stayed in Florida for therapy, because she had it three times a week. Once she got home, however, she lived her "normal" life again. Obviously, some tasks were harder with only one hand, but Blair learned to make it work. She thought about the attack all the time, how she didn't see it coming, how much it hurt, and how much it scared her. Blair wondered if she would ever get the guts to go scuba diving again, but she decided that one day she would try it again!

k
McFADDEN

Natalia Hart had been anticipating her role for months now. She couldn't wrap her mind around the thought of performing on the same stage as her idols once had. Taking the building's considerable age into account, Natalia relished in its historic significance. The play *Romeo and Juliet*, amongst others, had been performed there for nearly a century, and Natalia was fortunate enough to be the latest star granted the role of Juliet. Her idols, including Gemma Robinson, Kayla Laver, and Molly Lee, had blown away audiences in this role and earned their glorious fame. Natalia had to be utterly flawless. So she stayed after hours in the theatre, reviewing her lines over and over and over again.

Natalia will never forget the first night she decided to stay after hours. She read off "Wherefore art thou, Romeo?" and heard vague sounds of rustling or crawling near her feet. She decided it was probably a small animal of some sort. She knew the building was old and a perfect home for rodents. Natalia chose to shake it off, not wanting it to harm her performance with the distraction.

After she read on, Natalia decided to take a short break and replenish herself with the lemonade she brought in case her throat got dry. Before she took a sip, she noticed it had changed to a darker orange color. Natalia's paranoid mind realized it had been poisoned! Girl Scouts had forced her to learn how to identify poison years before. She was officially freaked out. She leaped off the stage and sprinted toward the exit.

Natalia's endeavor to vigorously shake the unexpectedly locked door failed. She purposely left it unlocked minutes before! She then ran down the hall to the dining room where high-class guests would pay extra to eat meals before the shows. She chose this room because she knew it had its own exit, and it was the nearest to her. Natalia normally acted quite gingerly amongst all the costly silverware and antiques in her view, but her conjecture that someone was after her caused her to leap from chair to chair to the next exit to avoid the tables in the way.

As Natalia laid her hand on the doorknob, a knife fell to the floor next to her. It must have been thrown! She violently turned her head to see who was there. As she rattled the locked door, she noticed no one was in the room with her. The lights began to flicker. Natalia realized the candles on the desk near her. She lunged to the nearest one to light it just in case. Natalia looked up at the detailed chandelier as the lights all went out, and all she had was that one single flame. She grasped the candle, knowing it was her only hope of getting out of the dark building.

Natalia heard the sounds of pouring rain just on the other side of the wall. On the other side of that wall was safety, her house, and people. Natalia was desperate! She refused to succumb to this evil being she thought was attacking her. She just wanted *out*! Natalia zigzagged down the complex halls that she had come to know so well in her months of rehearsing. Her last hope lay in front of her at the end of the last hall near the costume room. The last exit the theatre possessed was vital in this situation. Natalia stood upright with as much confidence as she could and shouted, "I need out...NOW!"

She took a deep breath and placed her palm on the handle, turned it softly, and pushed. Natalia was free! She had imagined before what she would do if she escaped. Now that was a reality, and Natalia needed to bring those thoughts to life. She had run away from whatever was keeping her hostage. Natalia dashed around the haunted theatre and was about to be on her way home when she noticed something. A cursory note was left on the dewy window of the theatre.

It stated, "I just wanted you back. Your forever love, Romeo."

jaden
MILLS

Eugene was sitting on the clear, white, sand beach bewildered by what he had just survived. He was holding his small satchel of supplies and staring straight out into the never-ending ocean, knowing his close friend was now past this world, or ocean in this case. Eugene chuckled a little bit at the irony of his companion, a deep-sea oceanographer, being buried deep in the ocean off the coast of Africa. When the last tip of the small airplane they were using for a science expedition went underwater, Eugene turned around to see the photographer that he was traveling with, Casey, laying across the beach with a heavy chest. Eugene rushed to his aid while opening his satchel, hoping he wouldn't be in permanent desolation. Before he could do anything, Casey sat up, and in short gasps, explained he had asthma. Eugene shoved his hand into his bag to see if it was holding an inhaler, only to realize half its contents were gone. After this discovery, he took a glance around to see three bags full of tripods, cameras, batteries, lenses, and all the camera equipment you could think of. He turned back to Casey with a baffled look. Eugene asked Casey if he realized the remarkable circumstances: his bags had survived because Eugene's bag was nearly empty. Casey, still struggling to regain his breath, nodded yes, shrugged, and managed to murmur the word "luck" with a small timid voice.

Although both of the both men had a huge interest in nature, neither had ever survived in the wilderness without some kind of help. Casey had some experience with camping, but he always had supplies. Somehow, even though both Casey and Eugene knew they had slim chances of surviving, neither of them broke down and gave up or went insane. Instead, they thought about what they needed to do first to survive. They very quickly made two mistakes: shedding some of their clothes and not making a fire. Although the blazing temperatures of Africa in the day made this rational, the temperature would drop by over 50 degrees at night. They also didn't think about the distillation of ocean water which needed a fire to work. They decided to trek back into the wilderness of Africa instead of surviving on the coast and making a dingy.

Casey, despite his asthma, decided to carry all three of his camera bags because of his devotion to the art of photography. Eugene didn't understand this devout determination driving Casey, but understood it somewhat because he sometimes felt the same way about science. Their first day was somewhat easy because they were still grateful for surviving the crash. However, the night was drastically different. They found a tall tree for shelter without thinking about its dangers. As the sun went down, Casey started taking pictures constantly. Eugene didn't mind as long as Casey didn't get injured or attract danger. With every picture Casey took, it was getting colder, and he was forced into the safety of the tree as soon as the last glimpse of the sun had slid past the long horizon.

In the middle of the night, Casey was awoken by the sound of a tripod falling over. He hesitantly and intelligently chose to stick in the tree, mainly because he was already cold enough, and the tree branches were acting as windbreakers. The next morning, Casey saw the tripod he had accidentally left out was knocked over with one of the legs gnawed on. He quickly showed Eugene, and they consciously agreed to move from their position for the next night. They also realized the importance of a fire at night. Their problems didn't end there. They were beginning to starve and above that, they were desperate for water. When they began to walk, they realized they had no idea where they were and no idea where the ocean was. Casey, based on instinct, moved towards the sun, but they still didn't know their location or direction.

Their simple walk to find a shelter turned into a mindless march, and it was wasn't long before they looked around to see a group of lions surrounding a carcass. Casey was the first to see them and quickly notified Eugene. They immediately stopped in their tracks and studied their surroundings. With Casey's talented eye of a photographer, he saw a full grown male black rhino standing in a bush staring directly at them both. Casey saw him and began to run, but Eugene only moved when the rhino was close enough to him that he could feel his footsteps. He escaped the horn's tip quickly, but had, in consequence, run even closer to the lions. The rhino turned right back around and refocused on its target, Eugene. It put down its head and massive horn and began to charge at full speed. Eugene easily ran out of the way of this charge and, in a stroke of luck, the lions fled when they saw the massive rhino charging towards them. The rhino continued to charge madly, which eventually turned into a sprint into the surrounding plain of land. When Eugene took another step, he felt a large splinter in his big toe but decided not to tell Casey because he didn't want him to worry. After Casey let out a yell for Eugene, they looked at each other and knew they weren't going to stay this lucky.

After the dust settled, Eugene studied the huge indistinguishable carcass in the area the lions were. The pair approached cautiously, and as soon as they could see any detail of the remains, they knew it was rotten and uneatable. The lions had obviously neglected and forgotten about the corpse which angered Casey. The anger was the first sign of his growing insanity which used his splinter as a fertilizer. As the sun dimmed, Casey started building a fire. Eugene explained the process, a beginners science technique, to Casey which was to simply take apart one of Casey's batteries and apply the steel wool he had in his bag to the positive side. They had a fire fairly quickly and returned to a tree for the night.

The second night was much easier than the first simply because they were more experienced. Casey had again taken pictures of the sunset, but that night, he set up a tripod to capture the early sunrise. When Eugene woke up in the morning, he noticed the tripod, which was again on the ground but still intact. He also noticed the markings on the ground which he quickly distinguished as hyena prints. Eugene advised Casey and they again decided to change locations.

After they relocated, their thirst and starvation began to set in. Casey was starved from three days without food, no water, and blazing heat. Eugene was too, but it was not as serious. With this dehydration came the possibility of insanity. Casey had already begun this process and was starting to say that the hyenas had stolen his cameras. Eugene was just far enough past sanity to think Casey was logical at the time. Their legs were now less like body parts and more like machines, made to drag their bodies from place to place. Even though their legs were suffering, their minds were worse. Their brains had passed this stage of suffering and fallen into a state of constant confusion. While on their mindless drag, they began to see illusions such as a tree full of fruit and an oasis of clean water. In both cases, they were tricked by their own minds. When Casey saw the fruit tree, he assumed it was carrying forbidden fruit and refused to get any closer, but Eugene tried to eat one and obviously failed by just grabbing for air. When they saw the oasis, they both ran to it and started drinking but ended up with a mouth of dirt.

When they settled down for the night, Casey setup again and started snapping pictures. With Casey's recent insanity came a false strength that made him stay up way later in the dangers of the safari. With Eugene's recent insanity came forgetfulness, so he didn't tell Casey to pack up and instead drifted off into a half sleeping and half dreaming state while resting on the branch of their newest tree home.

He was awoken by the chilling yell of the still awake Casey. Casey had been slashed far across the back by a hyena and had dropped to the ground in pain. The hyena fled when Casey yelled, and Eugene rushed to his aid. Eugene, half insane and adrenaline pumping, ripped his shirt off and wrapped the cloth around Casey's massive wound. Eugene dragged Casey to the tree and brought him up with the strength he had just been gifted by what seemed like a gallon of adrenaline. They both sat on the largest branch of the tree drifting off, Casey from blood loss, and Eugene from exhaustion.

Again, Eugene was awoken that night. This time, it was a search helicopter shining a bright light across the landscape. He shot up and out of the tree and started waving his hands now that his insanity had amazingly disappeared. The helicopter lowered the ladder, and Casey woke up to Eugene frantically dragging him from the tree. Eugene grabbed as many camera bags as he could but was forced to also help Casey up the ladder. He grabbed the tallest tripod with the nicest camera and started climbing the ladder with Casey right above him dripping blood everywhere from his back. With every rung of the ladder, Casey was getting weaker, and Eugene had to push harder up. By the time they reached the helicopter, Casey had almost passed out. The rescue team grabbed Casey and immediately started giving him medical aid. Eugene asked how the team found them, and the helicopter team replied saying Casey had a camera with a location device. Eugene asked Casey if he knew he had that camera. Casey, still struggling to regain his breath, shook his head no, shrugged and managed to murmur the word "luck" with a small timid voice.

O
MUYSKENS
The Cafe

Ding, the sound of the opening door rang throughout the small café. The proprietor stood in the corner, watching over his business with a despicable glower. Small talk pervaded the room, and a short line had gathered by the register. It stood out amid the turbulent and constant movement of the rest of the shop.

The man who had just walked in was tall, with dark hair and warm, brown eyes. As he walked in the door he almost tripped on the ledge, then he bumped into the person in front of him. Whenever someone came by him he would dodge them quickly and erratically, mostly resulting in more of a trip. When he got to the register, he ordered a plain black coffee, his words as quick and concise as anyone's had ever been. Once he placed his order, he pivoted on his heel and grimaced in pain and embarrassment as he spilled his hot coffee all over his dress shirt, staining the white silky fabric with a dark mark that stood out among his plain, boring style. He had also spilled his drink all over the brown-haired lady behind him. She flinched and turned towards the man.

"I-I'm sorry. I didn't mean to-I mean-I-I'm sorry," the man sputtered out awkwardly. The woman frowned.

"It's alright. I'm early to work anyway," she replied as she gingerly inspected the new stain on her blazer. She looked up, only to find the man briskly power-walking towards the bathroom. She shrugged blankly, ordered a chai latte, and sat down at a nearby table, where she grabbed a few napkins, as though nothing was amiss at all.

The man, however, was not as well-tempered. He muttered a speech of self-loathing all the way to the bathroom. When he finished scrubbing at his shirt with a nearby napkin, he left the restroom. Then he saw the woman, sitting at the table, the stain still there. He remembered the way he hadn't even offered her a napkin or anything. His impulsive actions haunted him. He had to do something to make it up to her.

He walked up to the counter and bought her a bagel. He had second thoughts the whole way, *What if she hated bagels? What if she already had one? What if she was allergic?* But he continued on with his quest and walked over to where she was sitting, sheepishly looking down at his feet, not knowing what to do or say. Thankfully, she acknowledged him.

"Is that for me?" she asked, smiling. The man nodded. "I'm sorry I bumped into you earlier," she continued.

"That would be my fault," the man said. He handed her the bagel. "I bumped into you, remember?"

"No, I just wasn't watching where I was going," the lady replied. The man looked up, surprised. He began to protest, insisting the coffee spilling was his doing, but the woman cut him off.

"I think I owe you a coffee. Plain black, right?" she asked, grinning.

The man stared at her for a moment, astounded. *How could she be so forgiving?* "Uh, yeah. That'd be nice actually." His face soon mirrored the woman's, and he was smiling just as big as she was. They walked up to the counter together, and they then ordered the man's coffee. When it was finished, the man stepped up to grab the coffee, but the woman stepped in front of him.

"Thank you," she said to the man behind the counter. The coffee boy nodded and got back to making coffee. She turned around and gave the drink-spiller a funny looking smile. "Maybe I should hold these," she joked. They both laughed. She gestured over to the table that she had been sitting at, and they took a seat. "So," the woman started, "I never did get your name."

The man swallowed some coffee. "I'm Alec," he said. "And you are...?"

"I'm Hazel," she replied. They looked up and smiled at each other, like fools in love.

r
OOI

It had been an interminably long time since I had been to the future. I chose to stay here because of her. It all began in mid-April when I received a message on my electrifying green watch telling me to see the boss. When I reached there riding on my Segway, I was told that I had to go to the past to fix a screwed-up girl, Ellie, and that I would act as her twin sister. The people who were managing my assignment assured me that they made it to where it would be as if I was with the family from the very beginning of Ellie's life. They would not notice the change, but I would. This was part of my assignment to graduate from the school I attended since I was five, but now I had to attend Ellie's high school using a pseudonym. It was vital for me to be discreet which would be easy to succumb to because I committed social suicide in the future a long time ago. But, if I could not fulfill this, I was going to be alienated from the future.

Attending school in a different time and place entranced me in the beginning, but reality hit when I arrived. The water fountains were starting to become covered in mold, the locker room was sodden with sweat, and the cafeteria reeked with meat that wasn't actually meat. When the first bell of the day rang, the halls became overly crowded with people precariously jostling each other.

I arrived at my first class, which was English. I sat behind Ellie, my sister. The English teacher introduced himself as Coach Wilson. He was an eccentric man who had an affection for green pens and comic books. Class began. I asked Ellie if I could see her schedule. I glanced over it, and apparently we had all the same classes. Class continued.

After school, we rode in a big ugly limo back home. Getting off, Ellie sauntered off into the woods near her house. She took out a match and a book titled CTBS. I watched in excruciating pain as she lit the book on fire. I was impelled to go on a tirade, but I decided to conceal my anger and watch. Where I came from, there weren't any physical books available to the public; they were all displayed in the few remaining museums. After a considerable amount of time passed, I decided to join rather than just watch.

Over time our friendship grew stronger. Ellie was not just a person that burned TCAP books, but she was also a friend. I continued to regularly attend school. After two years passed, I wondered if I should go back to the future, but I quickly rejected that thought. Even though, life was more complicated in this era; it was not peaceful in the future. Additionally, if I had gone back, I would have been filed as dead because with the technology available in the future, it's hard for anyone to get lost. I stayed in the past.

C
O'REILLY
Deep Down Under

It all started when Tim Jenkins and Phil Phillips were avidly scuba diving off of the coast of Miami, Florida just looking for some fun. They were at the ocean floor when something caught Phil's attention. The wet suits they were clad in had built in radios, so Phil radioed over to Tim and told him that he saw something. They ventured over towards the mysterious object. It turned out to be a sunken ship, so Phil and Tim swam up and down with excitement. They boarded and started to explore it. The ship was old and falling apart. The floor looked as if any moment it'd turn into ruins.

The ship seemed interminable till they finally got to the back where they found a bottle in the hand of a skeleton. He seemed to be the previous owner of the ship due to the sword that was in his other hand was engraved with the title captain. Their visit was cut short when they felt some turbulence from above. As soon as Tim and Phil got out of the sunken ship, the sand opened up and swallowed it like a monster, and all the artifacts went down with the ship.

When they reached the surface of the water, they saw a bunch of men in ski masks were intruding on their boat. The men on the boat spotted Tim and Phil and made a hasty getaway on a large speed boat. Tim and Phil were bewildered and had no clue of who would want to ransack their boat until Tim picked up a business card one of the men dropped. It belonged to one of the Brady Brothers. The brothers were the other scuba diving establishment from across Miami and were always trying to steal Tim and Phil's thunder. A couple years back, Tim and Phil were scuba diving when they came across a diamond and, the Brady brothers tried to take it while the two were sleeping. The two friends worked to get the boat running again to get back to shore.

The brothers raced back to the beach. They docked their boat and opened up the bottle that they had discovered on the sunken boat. It was a map and an old piece of paper that read "The treasure lies where all boats go to stay forever." There was a sandbar on the other side of Miami where a long time ago, boats would get stuck and never make it off so they ended up sinking. Tim and Phil used to dive over there till the police told them they couldn't dive there because of the dangers that lay below. Off the brothers went to the graveyard.

The two friends were stuck in traffic in the middle of the city when out of nowhere their car was rammed in the side by a van. Their car had suffered a considerable amount of damage to the outside, but it wasn't detrimental to the axle and the motor was still running. The Brady Brothers jumped out of their van and started trying to break the windows to get in. The brothers knew Tim and Phil had something important with them, and they wanted it. even though Tim and Phil had suffered a couple cuts and scrapes but weren't going to give it up that easily. Tim threw the car into reverse and sped away.

Tim and Phil were entranced with how fast the Brady Brothers figured out that they had a piece of history in their hands. They contemplated for a while about if they should just give up because this search was becoming dangerous, but they decided to carry on with the search because of the thrill of the adventure.

The two friends arrived at the beach that was about five miles from the boat graveyard. Tim and Phil were so caught up with the brothers, that they didn't think of a way to get out to the sand bar and get to the bottom to look for the treasure. There wasn't a trace of a boat nearby till out of nowhere they saw their long time friend Jon, a fellow scuba diver. They flagged him down and asked him if they could borrow his boat for the night. Jon was glad to let some scuba divers who share the same passion for the hobby borrow his boat, Overall the boat was in good shape although the seats were a little sodden. However, it wasn't desolated so they drove it out to the sand bar.

They got there and suited up in the diving suits Jon also let them borrow. They dove to the bottom where they set up a perimeter of where the treasure was supposed to be, then they got out their special underwater metal detectors, that had been lying around on the boat and Tim thought it might come in handy. Tim instantly got a ping from his metal detector, radioed over to Phil, and they started digging like mad men.

They had almost gone twenty feet deep when they hit something solid. Once they got it on the boat, they fervently opened it and uncovered that it was a chest, and an old one at that. As soon as they got it up to the boat and back to the shore, they opened it up. Inside was a diary and a couple pounds of golden coins. Inside the diary was the name Frederick Erickson, a famous prince from the 1800's who tried to assassinate his father but failed and was sent on a ship to the Bahamas, but the ship never made it. The two friends were amazed with the discovery they had just made.

Tim and Phil sold the chest they found to a museum that's in New York. With the money they received, they rebuilt their scuba diving business from the ground up. The two friends ended up making a name for themselves in the scuba business and were from there on out successful. On the other hand, the Brady Brothers ended up serving a 3 years sentence at the Miami, Florida State Penitentiary for reckless driving.

lillian e.
PARKER
Out of Sight, Out of Mind

"I hope Mr. Philson is nice."

"Well, I heard that he gives us essays every week."

"Someone told me that he never brushes his hair."

My eighth-grade English class at Virginia Robert Middle School began with irrelevant comments from my students, as always. This year's students weren't much different from previous years. For example, there were boneheaded jocks, the band geeks, the really smart kids, and all of the other groups in a regular middle school. I'm glad that my year was starting out to be calm and peaceful. I began to teach my first English lesson about our vocab units. Right off the bat I could see the exhilaration in some of my students, and the rest of my students were dreading the awful torture that "supposedly" I was putting them through. My year was starting out practically perfect! Well, it felt like that for weeks.

However, my affable nature soured when a new student, Lily Barker, transferred into my class. Lily was tantalizingly smart, and she spoke with great eloquence. The first day she came in my class, she knew everything about what I had to teach to my class; it was like she was the teacher. All of the boys fell head over heels for Lily, and ALL of the girls wanted to be her best friend. But *me*, I abhorred her. She was taking over my class by teaching my students the lesson of the day. For example, she always argued with me and told me my teaching methods were wrong, and I'm too lazy to kick her out of my class so I let her rant. She was also taking my pride by taking all of *my* spotlight away from me, the most glamorous teacher that is living on the Earth. NO! NO! Lily Barker was taking over my life. Because of her, I couldn't sleep at night. Something had to be done about this adversary of mine who always left me in deep consternation.

Soon enough, I did something to fix my problem with this derisive and demeaning eighth grade girl, Lily Barker. To start off my brilliant plan, I called her parents in for a parent-teacher conference, and they replied, "Yes. Of course." Next, I had put poison in a fruit drink that I offered to Lily and her parents at the beginning of the meeting. After their cups were empty, Mr. and Mrs. Barker fell to the floor, dead. Lily was bewildered as she realized what had happened, and what I had done because she was the last of the Barker's to drink the fruit punch. Soon after she realized what had happened, she also fell to the floor dead.

I DID IT! I completed my life-long goal! All of my suffering was over. I wanted to go brag about my accomplishment to my friends, so I did.

I skipped down the hallway happily to find my bestest friend in the whole wide world, Mr. Phillips. I was going to him to brag about my absolutely amazing accomplishment. When I got into his bright room with posters all around, I screamed "I KILLED LILY BARKER! AND I DID IT WITHOUT ANY HELP!" Once I said that I knew I shouldn't have. Mr. Phillips was so mortified that he started to cry like a baby when he heard my awesome news. I was in shock that he didn't like what I did or what I said. Instead, he shoved me into his work office, and while I was in there, he called the police.

His office was old, filled with dingy lab coats, and a freezer filled with dead frogs that left a gruesome smell in my nose. I passed out because the smell was so horrifyingly bad. When I woke up, a big fat police man was in my face trying to drag me out of this closet.

Soon enough, the police put me into a bright red and blue police car and took me away to a nice shiny new jail cell all for me and only for me. That plump police man told me that I was in here for a life sentence with a charge of murder. I'm not sad or mad that I am in here; I'm happy because my goal is complete. I have no guilt for what I did. I aimed at it, and I achieved my goal: to kill Lily Barker.

abbey
PHILLIPS
The Drowning

Picking the local newspaper up off of her front lawn, Ms. Wilson, an abnormally fit 85-year-old woman, looked at the date and reassured herself that today was the day. She went about her morning routine, which included taking a shower, brushing her hair and teeth, and then eating breakfast. When she was finished, she got into her car and drove to the animal shelter. Clad in a black sweater and dark pants, she walked into the shelter in a discreet manner, going unnoticed by the people surrounding her and the employees on duty.

She quickly walked to where the newborn puppies were located, picked three at random, and placed them in the duffel bag she was carrying on her shoulder, so she could more easily take them to the river. Once again, her presence going unnoticed, or so she thought, she left the building, fumbling with her keys as she hurried towards her car. She located a nearby river with a map, and when she heard the rushing water, she pulled over and stopped the car. It was time. Ms. Wilson took a deep breath and sat upright in her seat. She looked in the rearview mirror and concealed her fear of being caught with a malicious grin.

Finally working up the courage to get out of the car, Ms. Wilson grabbed the duffel bag of squirming puppies and headed towards the river. She scanned the area with a wary glance, but soon got to work. She remembered the dog attacking her in seventh grade. It bared its teeth and sunk them deep into her flesh, leaving a permanent scar all the way up her forearm. Ms. Wilson grabbed the first one, looking it over, and frowning in disgust because it resembled the dog that bit her in the past so closely. She plunged the puppy underwater, taking its life. She did the same to the second, but just as she was going to drown the third puppy, she saw the blue and red flashing lights in her peripheral vision. The squealing of the sirens was so deafening, Ms. Wilson could barely hear the voice of the policeman, who was jumping out of the car.

"PUT YOUR HANDS WHERE I CAN SEE THEM!" the officer screamed. "What the heck are you doing?!?" he asked, appalled and bewildered at the sight of an elderly woman drowning puppies. Shocked that someone had actually seen her, Ms. Wilson backed away with the fear that she once had at the beginning of her plan. As she called for backup, Ms. Wilson, strangely being as fit as a teenage athlete, tried to make a dash towards her car. The policeman turned to see her trying to get away and did what he had to do. Not knowing the age of the culprit, he had anticipated something like this would happen, so he tased her. Numb from the shock, Ms. Wilson fell to the ground with a thud.

When backup finally arrived, they thought she was dead and carried her limp body to the police car. They drove her to the station where the doctors, who were on the way from the hospital, and police chief would first make sure she was alive, and then, if she was, they would decide her fate: prison or a mental institute. Strangely enough, she was alive, and her test results diagnosed her as mentally insane. She was sent to the institute. Once the police van arrived at the institute, she was placed in a room with white walls and a simple bed. They only let her out of the room for meals and using the restroom. She stayed there for two weeks and did the same thing every day...before the accident happened.

One day, at 12:30 p.m., it was lunchtime for Ms. Wilson, and she was getting ready for the same, bland meal of some kind of soggy meat and a glass of water. While she was walking up the stairs to the cafeteria, a patient, who looked considerably younger than her, gave her a rather dismissive look. This happened invariably because many of the patients had heard what she did to the puppies, making it impossible to not notice the looks. She sat down in the most remote part of the cafeteria and looked at the sodden meat in front of her. Noticing the amount of other mad people around her, she started to wonder what they did to end up here. She was hesitant at first because they could have been harmless, but soon felt threatened by the lingering glares, knowing that other patients could attack at any second.

She felt the neglect from the authority figures who worked at the hospital. She knew the only place she was safe was locked away in her room. Ms. Wilson got up, threw her food away, and walked towards the door leading to the stairs. It wasn't long before she heard footsteps behind her. She turned to see who it was was, but she only heard a derisive laugh and saw the familiar dismissive, scornful look as she was pushed down the stairs.

When the ambulance arrived, she was strapped to a gurney. They arrived at the hospital minutes later. The hospital lights flashed as she was rushed through the emergency room. They tried to help her, but nothing could be done to save her. Ms. Wilson had broken her neck and stopped breathing as soon as she fell. The institute didn't want the truth to get out about what had actually happened. It could make them look as if they weren't paying attention to their patients. In turn, the institute lied to her family about what had happened to Ms. Wilson and told them she had suffered a heart attack because of anxiety. The institute held a funeral, and the family and friends of Ms. Wilson were all invited to mourn her unfortunate death, although they didn't know the truth. Still, the news spread of the puppy incident, and no one, not even the family, attended.

j
RATHERT
Robbery

It was a cold night in Kentucky as I scouted the walls of the top-notch U.S. military base. The base was Fort Knox, a U.S. bullion depository for gold. I, Ilya Rinne, was an ex-special forces operator from the Kommando Spezialkräfte. A few other ex-special forces members and I, spanning from eastern Ukraine, Jaromigr Reznov, and the southern U.S., Tyler Bryzgalov who was ex-Spetsnaz and moved to southern Alabama, teamed up to deprive the U.S. of part of their gold. Our team also consisted of Teemu Lundqvist, ex-Särskilda Skyddsgruppen, Jaküb Wojciech, ex-JW Grom, and Patrice Voracek, ex-Joint Task Force 2. The man who made the plans was Evgeni Yakupov, ex-Jagdkommando.

We all wanted revenge for being wrongfully discharged from our military branch. We were all discharged for apparently not providing enough protection to Meir Kahane, a controversial American-Israeli Rabbi, while he was visiting Iraq, and I was on tour as his guide. He was almost killed by a group of local terrorists, because a majority of people did not care for him. We decided to start with the U.S., because it would let the world know who we are and what we are capable of. Although I was discharged in 1990, it was still angering me even eight years later. It was a demeaning thought, as I always wanted to protect my country.

The plan was simple: get in and get out cleanly, using a pair of bolt cutters to cut down the fence surrounding us. No man left behind, and leave no evidence. It wasn't a concise plan. We had simulated and evaluated the mission 100 times, and there was 25% of not making it out alive. That idea was rebuffed by 4/6 though as they began to place more advanced security around the edges of the 170 mile^2 base. At the last minute, I suggested another idea, and that was to rappel in through a helicopter. So we agreed on it, and purchased a decommissioned UH-1H Iroquois, or more commonly known as the Huey, for the job. We would still have to work out how to evade guards as there were about 8,000 people working and living there. We soon also purchased camouflaged gear to carry supplies, obtained explosives needed, and painted the helicopter to meet U.S. military standards to stay anonymous.

The mission began at 2300 hours at a private airstrip near Elizabethtown, Kentucky. We were flown a few dozen miles north, and then we were dropped off right inside of the base after entering the military airspace as a helicopter part of a nighttime practice raid. My team walked gingerly, and prepared ourselves for any attacks (if any were to happen). We were able to get a few hundred yards without any disturbances. That was until we heard the sounds of what could've been someone tapping water. We hit the ground immediately, hoping that we were not compromised. We paused and waited a few minutes to see if the sound appeared again. It didn't appear again, but we did see cadets practicing target shooting with suppressors. That was probably the cause of the noise.

We carried on after, sticking to the shadows to guarantee that we would not be seen. We were almost spotted though, as a convoy practicing nighttime raids drove by us. We quickly leapt behind some empty oil barrels for cover. The convoy was very long, and it took it a few minutes to pass by us. After, we picked up the pace and soon came within ½ a mile of the storage compound. There were more guards working at night than the daytime, so we had to be very careful. We crawled the rest of the way there, like a snake going in for the kill. The grass moved very slightly as we crawled through it. It was 0200 when we finally reached the compound, and busted off the lock. My squadron snuck inside, and we were greeted by crates of golden bars. We quickly gathered as much as possible and lined the ones we were not able to grab with C4. It was now 0230, so we finished up and tried to exit quietly, but we were "greeted" by a guard.

He was shocked, and so were we. He tried reaching for his gun, but Patrice quickly lunged at him and began a fight with him. He dragged him inside to reduce the risk of being heard by the guards, who were heavily armed. We left the guard gasping for air as Patrice punched him in the neck. Some guards, however, were alerted by the noise of us dragging him inside, and they started to investigate, so we had to go out the backdoor. The bullets whizzed by us, and I winced at every round fired. We continued to run even though one of my comrades, Jaküb, was shot and captured. We began to get closer and closer to the rendezvous point and I heard a helicopter approaching. I looked around and became very tremulous. It was ours, but it was immediately shot down by a nearby air defense. Both Evgeni and Jaromigr were in it, and most likely dead.

I quickened my pace even though my heart was about to burst. I knew I was close, but the guards were gaining on me. I was closing in on the barrier, about 50 yards away. To provide a distraction, I detonated the bombs planted in the facility holding the gold. It was a turbulent site of the former gold storage. My escape vehicle was gone, so I had to improvise. I heard a military truck approaching, and decided to use it to my advantage. As it quickly passed by us trying to hit us, I grabbed a hold of the front door. I opened it, and tried to pull the driver out. It took a bit of work as he was still tightly buckled in, but I managed to throw him out. I turned the car around and headed towards the remaining group. I stopped for a split-second and picked them up. The truck easily broke down the chain-link fence encompassing us from freedom. When I broke free of the compound, I gunned the truck to 80 mph, and the pursuers began to fall back.

After the authorities were left far behind, we stopped at an abandoned house along Interstate 65 to count the amount of gold stolen. We counted out the cost of the gold, and it amounted to $50M. We evenly split the money between the remaining 4 of and decided on which target to attack next. The Germans gold reserve.

a
REYNOLDS

As I pulled into the school's parking lot, it looked so empty compared to it usually being full of cars. The emptiness made me even more scared for what I was about to do. I had to go back to the school to retrieve my cellphone, which I had accidentally left there earlier that day. Not having my phone was driving me up a wall because I wasn't able to talk to my friends or do my usual internet surfing like I was used to. However, I was terrified to go there at night because of the rumors about a ghost that haunted the school. Most say the ghost's name was "Emilie," and that she wandered the halls from sunset to sunrise. Others said that at night she appears in the windows and lurks among the humans that live around the school. Yet, despite the stories, I knew what I needed to do. I needed to go back to the school to get my phone.

After I gathered enough courage up to get out of my car, I began to walk towards the school, praying that the doors would still be unlocked. The trees' leaves whispered amongst themselves, as if they were trying to warn me about something. My stomach tied itself in knots as I reached the building. I looked inside the pitch black school, which was so different than the usual bright and busy nature of it. I gulped, hesitantly grabbed the door handle, and pushed the door open; however, my previous prayers proved to be useless because the door was locked. I turned around and began to walk back towards my car.

Click!

The areas around me were silent, so I knew the sound I heard had to be the doors unlocking. I slowly walked back towards the door, and as I reached for the door's handle, in my peripheral vision I saw something shining in the distance. I looked up as quickly as I could, but before my eyes could adjust, the light had disappeared. *Am I just imagining this?* I felt like I was going mad, but despite my fears, I avidly wanted to get my phone back.

I opened the door and followed the path that would lead me to my last period of the day, which was Mr. Brown's English class, which was where I believed I left my phone. It was so dark, but I had to find my way. I kept going straight, and I was eventually able to feel around a wall and find a light switch. I flicked it on, and I looked up the steps that were right in front of me. At the top of the stairs, I saw something I could never forget. I saw a tiny, emaciated little girl, wearing an elaborate night gown, which was dirty and white with lace embroidering its edges. This looked like it wasn't her first trip on the stairs before. *Could it be her?*... There was no way. Either way, I spoke out and said, "Hello? Who are you?"

With no answer, no response, and no movement from the little girl, I began to walk up towards her. My adrenaline was pumping, and I felt fearless. As a result of my fearlessness I reached out and tried to touch her, still in shock by this all. I wanted to see if she was real, so when I was close enough, I touched her arm, and it was stiff and cold. I jerked my hand away and gasped. When I did so, she disappeared. I ran up the last few steps, and I was now not only on a journey to find my phone, but I was also in search of the little girl.

The lights I had turned on earlier had clicked off, probably having something to do with my recent ghost encounter, and I was in total darkness once again. I struggled to see anything; however, not too far off, I saw a dim glow. Presuming it may have been *her*, I began to follow it. She was moving at a much faster pace than me, so it was difficult to keep up. I soon lost track of her and began to panic. I tripped and fell in the struggle to find light, and I hit my head on something hard near me. I felt around to try to figure out what it was. After my eyes adjusted a bit more, I was able to make out what the object was. It seemed to be a medium sized chest that looked centuries old. The wood it was made from looked somewhat rotten and discolored. *What is this doing here?*

Feeling terrorized, I looked around the hall in a quick manner to look for a light switch. Lucky to find one so quickly, I turned it on and hurried back over to the newly revealed chest. I opened it to find a body, and strangely enough, it looked just like the little girl, from the hair to the dingy clothing. After I actually realized what I had found, I felt the air thicken, and it was hard to breathe. I started to panic because of the chest, and the thought that this may just all be a hallucination. I stumbled away from the chest as I ran to a nearby classroom, and I shut the door behind me, but also making sure to flick on a light as I entered the room. I looked around the classroom, and luckily it was Mr. Brown's room. The phone was sitting on his desk. I snatched it, ran down the hallway, and darted out of the school. I stopped for a second once I was at my car to take a look at the dim school. *Thank God I wouldn't be alone there tomorrow.*

andrew
ROBINSON
Hawthorne

It was just a normal day in The Bear's Den, the local grub joint. It was as busy as it gets when the town's population can all be gathered up in two hundred square feet, if that tells you anything about the size of Rust, the town we call home. At the restaurant, there were a few families sittin' down for a nice ol' home-cooked meal and some Coke. Some men were spending their hard earned paychecks on some of the best food for miles around. The cooks were fixin' up food the only way they knew how: the right way. The servers were merely somethin' easy on the eyes and that's all; not good at their job, but the customers sure do like 'em. The Sheriff and his deputy were sitting at the bar, each havin' a glass of whiskey. Everyone was having a good time. Shoot, even I was having a good time playing games with my brother, and I ain't one to play games, let me tell you.

That was until he walked in, clad in a white suit with white pants and a little red bow tie. His name's James Hawthorne, and he's a con man. Conned pretty much everybody in this little town. To put it simply, he's not welcome here.

"What're you doing here, you despicable little recluse? You know you aren't welcome in this town!" scathingly yelled Old Miss Anne, one of the cooks. Scornful, scathing shouts were cast from the crowd and reverberated around the entire room. He tried his hardest not to react. Hawthorne avoided the hate and walked over to the bar. The bartender ignored him.

When my brother and I gained the courage to talk to the despondent man, we asked what he was doin' in this city.

"I'm dyin', I got this rare disease and now I'm dyin'," he said to us vaguely and coughed in a very odd way. "I just want to come back and make right what I've done to y'all."

"What's this 'rare disease' called anyways?" He didn't look ill, so I didn't believe him until he named the disease to be some rare form of lung cancer that I haven't even remotely heard of and handed over a doctor's note when we asked him for more proof. It sounded quite gruesome though. I felt terrible. We told everybody that they should be ashamed with the way they were acting and that we've got a dyin' man on our hands. We escorted the sick man out of there and offered him a place to stay, but he said he's already staying some place.

It wasn't until our ears were pressed to his motel room's door that we discovered he actually was fakin' it. My brother and I were walkin' by his room to bring him a gift and expected the usual heavy coughing, but he was talkin' clear as day to some man about his 'master plan.'

"Now I don't care a bit if it's wrong. You will pull as many cons on as many folks as you can, or I will fire you without giving you any sort of cut of the money; you got that through that thick skull of yours?" James yelled at an unknowing pawn whom we didn't know. The revelation sure came as a shock to me. He opened the door, and we fell into the room. We made a run for it, but I think Hawthorne still caught a glimpse of me. "After them, you fool!" he yelled once again at his minion. We ran down the two flights of stairs as fast as we could. Once we was out, my brother got in the car and started it while I ran around out back, leading them away from him so my brother would have the time to start the car. Right when I thought I was caught, my brother pulled the car right up and slowed down just enough so that I could get in. We left our chasers eating our dust and boy, was it amazin'. I'd hate to be watching from his perspective. Little did we know what was to happen.

On our way back into town, we noticed a guy was following us. I turned around, and it was the same guy we saw at the motel. We were just barely ahead of him the entire time. Our car was better than his, hands down, but he was somehow gaining on us. After a minute, we heard a loud bang. Either his engine had blown out, or he was shootin' at us. Hopefully the former. Another loud noise, and our back windshield was cracked, which confirmed our suspicion of gunfire.

Two more shots, and these were more rapid. Glass from our back window went everywhere. When we slowed down, our little chaser cut us off and would've stopped us in our tracks. All the luck in the world must have been used there and then, because by some miracle, he kept on drivin', right off the road and into the stream. On top of that, he stopped shooting when he got out! We'd lost him with all our limbs where they needed to be.

By the time we'd tried to convince everyone that ol' James was only fakin' it, he'd managed to gain the affections of everybody in town, and it was all our fault for telling them lies. It was too late for anyone to believe us.

"What if we make him confess to everybody that he ain't sick?" proposed my brother.

"Naw, he'd never go for it," I replied.

"He might if we was to trick the confession out of him."

I stopped for a moment. "Hey, that might just work! Only one problem, how are we supposed to do that?" And so we talked for about two hours before coming up with a somewhat elaborate gambit of a plan which would be completed that very night.

* * *

"Okay, be as quiet as you can now. We just need to discreetly slip this paper on his desk, take the distributor cap from his engine, and we've got this scam in the bag,"

I said as we crept through the candle-lit halls of the newly built motel.

"What's that paper say anyhow?" asked my brother.

"That's irrelevant. Just go remove the distributor cap from his car. Hurry, before he gets back here!" And on that note, my brother left. Now it was up to me to plant the note while we thought Hawthorne was in the lobby getting his mail. His room was dark, so I flipped on the light switch. I walked over to his desk which had his stationery, some bills, loose change and the tantalizing remnants of a small meal on it. I stopped to look at a paper which was sittin' on his desk for a minute. It was an austere letter to his partner in crime. That could be our evidence! I quickly retrieved it, pocketed it, and ran to the door. However, something went amiss, because I turned around only to find James sitting upright in his chair grimacing at me as I frantically and tremulously hastened to get out of the room. How could I have overlooked that mail doesn't come on weekends? I scrambled to open the door and quickly turned out the lights before I left, in the hopes that he wouldn't get out of his room quick. I ran down the stairs as fast as I could and suddenly heard a door slam shut behind me. A few seconds later, I was out of the building and runnin' to my brother, who had almost finished his part. He saw me running and knew just what to do. He wrenched some other parts out of Hawthorne's vehicle and took a run for our getaway car, and I was not far behind. We had already taken off when Hawthorne got out of the motel.

I read the letter aloud to my brother while we drove about four blocks up and two to the left to the sheriff's office and gave him the letter.

"Well, I'll be darned!" he said, bewildered. "I'll have this sent right over to the mayor, and we can have this 'examined.' Thank you two boys for this information, you'll probably be called over to the courthouse real soon so we can hear your side of the story."

"Okay, thank you, officer." With that, we left, but not without relishing in the moment.

About five hours later, the mayor made an announcement about James Hawthorne being a fraud. He was forced to make a confession and apology, return all the money his henchman stole and on top of all that, they were both arrested. I have a feeling this is the last we'll be seeing of ol' James around here.

The girl sat up gingerly, slowly observing her surroundings. She rubbed her eyes and gathered the scraps of the blanket encompassing her on the ratty mattress. A thin ray of light filtered through the window and down onto the ground, illuminating the grimy floor covered in dust and stains. Her mother was nowhere to be seen; she was invariably working. Unable to pay taxes, they were forced to borrow money from a loan shark. Their deadline to the debtor was soon, so her mother was forced to work more. The girl sighed and stood up, rubbing her limbs to life from the cold. The light was blocked by the tall office building - the opposite of the small and cramped flat they lived in - so she used her hands to guide her in the dim light, crawling through the doorway and into the back street. She covered her eyes from the street lights and plodded into a dark alleyway, jumping over puddles and sliding against walls. Her foot caught on something and she heard a small groan, startling her and making her speed up. Heart beating erratically, she reached the entrance of the dingy passageway and looked upon the littered street.

The body of another person clad in garbage sat across from where she stood, too weak to stand or even to beg for kindness from the irascible, cold people passing by.

She averted her eyes from the tremulous figure and hurried down the sidewalk, looking down at the ground. The girl made her way down to the cement colored building where a line of people stood, waiting. Edging her way through the soup kitchen's doors and into the crowd, she found herself a place and took a tray. Grabbing everything edible she was allowed, she gobbled the bland food down, pocketed some biscuits without anyone noticing, and quickly returned to the street, passing by the weak, pitiful person again and continuing down another alleyway.

The Dumpsters lining the back alley that she often visited were rich with rubbish. The girl scavenged through them trying to find tidbits she could "resell," tossing unneeded scraps aside while favoring others. She quickly came up with a pile of plastic toys and knickknacks, and with the remains of cardboard and cloth, tied them all together and slung it over her back so she only had to take one trip. She froze as she heard a loud voice near her. The girl quickly stilled and kept quiet as the person complained loudly. Her skin crackled with electricity as she heard them protest and grumble about the people lining the streets. "Why can't they just get jobs? They're so lazy; they just sit around all day and beg."

"They make our city look bad by being here," another voice agreed. The girl gripped the bundle close to her, her face inflamed. She bit her tongue to keep her from yelling out as the speakers' voices faded away. She buried her grimacing face into her arms, and her nails

THIS WAS A GRADE.

tore into her flesh. Ignoring the excruciating pain, she stood up quietly and walked despondently back down the bleak alley to her home, her shadowed face afflicted. The girl walked to the flat, her mouth sticking shut from her lips pressing together. Her footsteps echoed through the hallway as flies buzzed beside the spilled trash bins. She threw herself into the door and fell into the entryway, dragging herself to the bedroom. She collapsed on the bed and squeezed her eyes tightly.

j
SANDS
Wrecked

It was a bleak, rainy day, the ground sodden with water. Janie and I were in last block at Eleanor Lee High School. The school day felt interminable, especially that day. It was apparent we were both excited for what was in store for us later that night. We were going to see the premier of *Mockingjay Part One*.

We saw *The Hunger Games* and *Catching Fire*. Then, part one of *Mockingjay* came out. The premier was at our local movie theater at midnight. The cool settings and intense action is what drew us in and is the reason why we love the series so much. Every day we both checked our Twitter, Facebook, and Instagram for updates on the new release. We even got matching t-shirts for that night. At lunch, in between classes, and during our free time in class, we would go over what was going to happen when we got there and what characters were our favorite.

Finally, the bell rang, and Janie and I rushed out of class toward the main entrance of the school. After we exited the school, we got into Janie's car, me driving and her in the passenger seat. As we headed to her house, we passed Smoothie King, the best, yet most expensive, smoothie place in town. We succumbed to getting a medium sized smoothie for each of us. Then, we got back into the car and on the road. We started crossing an intersection on Jameson Street, and that's when my life changed forever.

A huge red truck came barreling towards the side of Janie's car and rammed into the passenger side. The cadence of smashing and breaking car parts and glass overwhelmed my ears. Between the high pitched shattering glass and deep crushing of metal, I felt like I was in an explosion. The collision happened in a matter of seconds, and it was hard to comprehend what and how it actually happened. There were traces of blood on the dashboard and broken pieces of glass. I became frantic and tremulous and got out of the wreckage as fast as I could. That's when I remembered Janie.

I ran over to the passenger side and called out her name, trying to extricate her body from the car. Many cars had stopped to see what happened and to come help us. A lady had seen what happened and called 911 for help. While people were helping me get Janie out, the police and an ambulance arrived at the scene, reassuring me that Janie was going to be okay. The paramedics finally got Janie out after many attempts and lifted her onto a gurney and into the ambulance. I followed, watching her unconscious body. The man driving the big truck was not harmed in any way and apologized, but I didn't want to accept his apology. I was apprehensive that she was not going to be okay, so I entreated the paramedic to let me come in the ambulance too. Sadly, they told me only family could ride with her. I called my mom to come pick me up, and luckily it only took her eight minutes to arrive since she was home.

We got to the hospital, and my mom dropped me off, leaving me standing nervously at the lobby entrance. I wanted to go in, but at the same time I felt that I wouldn't be able to handle any bad news. I stood there a good five minutes contemplating it, but finally decided to go in. As I walked into the hospital, many doctors and staff members looked heart broken. I guess the hospital had called Janie's parents earlier, because they were sitting next to each other, tears streaming down their faces. One of the paramedics that had taken Janie away walked up to me and placed his hands on my shoulders and told me that Janie had passed away. I couldn't believe that I had just lost my best friend. In a matter of seconds, tears began to roll down my face.

SPROUSE
The Teacher from Ipanema

It had finally come upon us. The largely underrated, hugely overlooked Free Comic Book Day for 2014 was here, and I was way beyond excited because I didn't know what nerderific plans were ahead of me. All I did know was that they were going to be great. That morning, I made sure I wore as much comic-themed clothing as possible including a Shazzam T-Shirt, B@Man high-tops, and an Amber Lantern ring. From the start, it was obvious that I was going to relish every bit of that day.

Free Comic Book Day is a one-day event where comic shops all across North America and even the World hold huge, nerdy events, and give away select comic books for free. It exists to help enlarge the fan base of comic nerd culture because comic nerds are on the endangered species list...probably. Nerds and their adored fandoms also make up a good-sized portion of the economy, so losing us or the things we invest ourselves into would hit everyone's pockets hard.

Anyways, Papa Sprouse and I had planned on going to as many comic shops in the Nashville area as possible until we got tired. We wanted to get the most out of our Free Comic Day experience that year. One shop, however, stuck out not because of the shop's quality, but because of an exhilarating and fearful event that took place in between those walls. The name of that comic shop was Comic Town, located in Belmont, Massachusetts.

By this point of the day, we had a hazy, unspecified rhythm to what we were doing. We'd walk in, be polite to the employees, maybe catch up with some familiar faces that we saw, retrieve our comics, and leave. There was nothing else to it. But this place was slightly different. Papa Sprouse and I walked into Comic Town, and so far, we were following the plan. The employees greeted us with delight, and instead of immediately getting our comics, they informed us of their main attraction for that day: "Geek Jeopardy." They explained that it was a geeky rendition of a popular trivia game-show named *Jeopardy*. Instead of lame topics like politics and weird vocabulary, "Geek Jeopardy" uses topics like *Star Wars* or *Teen Titans*. It seemed fairly simple and exceedingly enjoyable, so Papa Sprouse and I both eagerly signed up for our chance to play the game.

After we signed up, the two of us strolled through the diverse collection of nerdy memorabilia such as a stormtrooper piggy-bank, a *Detective Comics* #27 poster, a lonesome, bearded, 8th grade English teacher action figure, the 4th Doctor's scarf, and a *Star Trek: The Next Generation* series phaser. Every once in a while, you could distinctly hear the pronunciation of the next trio of contestants for "Geek Jeopardy." One round though, the host of the game kept calling out names, but no one was present. All of the people who had signed up to play had already left. The room grew hopeless until I heard the host summon a familiar name: Henry Sprouse.

I gathered myself together and walked up to the stage. Most of the categories seemed rather familiar. It had felt like the nerditude had just jumped right out of me. But what made it even better was when the man that was 5% beard, 95% pain was called up. His name was Jake from State Farm, but he told me to call him by his stage name: Jake Wilson. The spot light had come down on us, and so much was expected. Strangely, it reminded me of *High School Musical.*

We were placed next to another young, female nerd, and by the looks of her apparel, she seemed to be strictly from the SuperWhomLock (a mash-up of *Super Nature*, *Doctor Whom*, and *Pick-Lock* collaborated by Tumble users) fandom. As much as SuperWhomLock BookFace feed annoys me, I still respected her life choices because all of us nerds have made eccentric decisions about our time usage before. Except for me. All of mine are completely and utterly the most practical and efficient ways to spend time.

Anyways, the categories for "Geek Jeopardy" were revealed and were as followed: *Star Wars*, Cap-Com, *Teen Titans*, *Harry Potter*, and Famous Pilots in the Nerdy Universe. The game had begun. Jake had had first pick of which question to choose first, and after he hoarsely growled out Cap-Com, I knew I was in for trouble. His presence was too overwhelming in the most competent way possible. His eyes were glowing with rage like fire, and his beard sardonically judged me an invariable amount of times as if it was an omniscient being standing high above. Except it wasn't. I was of course.

The rest of the game was a slow blur as Jake from State Farm took high command of the makeshift scoreboard. I barely even noticed when the host revealed Jake Wilson as winner; I was so caught up in the thrill of Free Comic Book Day. Because on Free Comic Book Day, everyone is a winner. While I was consulting with Jake about his win, I vaguely remembered seeing a slip of paper sticking out of his side pocket that read "Reading Analysis." It was then that Jake from State Farm's campaign for darkness had begun. To all who are enrolled in his class: say goodbye to your hopes and dreams.

d
STOLZ

As I wake up, I wince at the pain of my stinging sunburn from forgetting to apply sunscreen the previous day. I frantically hasten to get dressed in my clothes as I get prepared for this Easter Sunday. I get in my mom's car and try to anticipate who is going to find the golden egg. My friends and I will all be hunting for eggs on the farm where we keep our horses. We arrive at the farm where the egg hunt will take place. I am going to get my stubborn, medium sized horse, Ruger, and saddle up since we will be riding for the hunt. After my friends, Deanna, Lindsey, Beth, Kayla, a few others, and I are ready, we are released to find the eggs, and most of all the golden egg.

Minutes after we are released to the front yard of the owner's property, I see the thing that we are avid for. My erratic friends overlook the egg. As I make my way, on horseback, to the golden egg, my horse reaches down and picks it up with his mouth, probably thinking it was a treat. I surmise that he is about to attempt to chew and swallow it, so I hurriedly get off and endeavor to get him to give it back. My intention is to precisely grab the egg he had gotten ahold of. Of course it is inevitable that I would have to fight for it.

Finally, he lets go of the egg. It just so happens that I had mistaken a plain yellow egg, with only twenty five cents, for the golden one that contained $100! I mounted back onto my horse and started to ride over to my friends to tell them what just happened. All of a sudden, I heard someone yell, "I found it, I found it!" Defeated by my friend Deanna, we head back to our parents, where there are racing games set up. As my friends are complaining I am left shocked by the fact that I didn't find the most important egg. The parents elaborate on the rules and then give more information that was irrelevant for what we had to do in order to win the games. As you can probably guess, I lost those too. Today was the first of the annual egg hunts my friends and I have started.

d
SUTHERLAND
YMCA Shark Pit

Dreams can be confusing. One night you're in the darkness of a city finding villains and crooks, and the next night it's in your local community pool. One of my dreams was one of the latter, but it was no normal pool trip.

So, this particular night, I was around six or seven years old and fell asleep feeling content, not even aware of the supposed "dangers" that were in this dream. I finally drifted off, and the dream ensued. Now, most, if not all, of my dreams are in third person. That is how I will tell this story.

My name is Timmy, and I am not so important but to play the main part in this story. I don't talk a lot in my dreams, if at all, so I am not as important as you would think. The setting was my local pool, sometime around 2006. My pool had a four foot deep end and went up until you reached the surface, about two feet from the wall, which had a few benches at the edge of it. It also had a frog slide on the right side of it looking from the wall. Also, this was a dream, so the size of anything wouldn't have that much effect on the objects that are in the dream. With all of that said, let's finally let the story commence.

"Mom! Dad!" Timmy yelled, "Look at the water!" There were loads of kids safely in their parents' arms, because something had happened in the pool. It had been filled to the brim with sharks! The parents were scared, and rightfully so. However, the sharks seemed friendly enough. Timmy's mom and dad looked at each other and both knew that they were thinking the same thing: we cannot allow him to go into that pool.

"Please, Mom? You've always let me do what I want, like the time I ate all of that candy and you didn't even try to stop me! Why can't I do that now?" Timmy asked.

His mom immediately replied, "Because those sharks are deadly and dangerous!" Timmy started to get mad, but then he saw something out of the corner of his eye. Or, rather, he saw an eye out of the corner of his eye. He gasped as he saw what looked like a hammer in the water. But it couldn't have been a hammer! That place was filled to the gills with sharks! But the idea was tantalizing. A shark that looked like a hammer? Impossible! He tried to goad his brain into thinking about something else. Meanwhile, his parents were giving in to the pungent smell of shark skin.

Timmy walked up and said, "Mom? Are there any sharks that look like hammers?" He said this with such wonder and awe, it bewildered her for a few seconds. She winced and thought, knowing that he was talking about the pool.

"Well...there's one called a hammerhead."

With this knowledge, Timmy asked if he could go in again.

She hesitated and said, "Oh, all right. What harm could it do? Right?" Suddenly thoughts of an frail and emaciated looking Timmy flashed through her brain. She jumped up to stop him, but it was too late. He was up on the frog slide, already going down into the sea of swarming sharks. She began to shed tears in agony, thinking that she would never see her boy again. She became hoarse, and Timmy's father leaned next to her and, without being told, obediently started comforting her. A man knows what to do in that situation. He subtlety soothed her just in time to wearily look up and saw Timmy riding the hammerhead with a gleam in his eye and an affectionate smile on his face.

Timmy was in perpetual joy, invariable happiness, and best of all, while his clothes were sodden, he was alive! His mom couldn't have been happier. She sat upright and waved to him, and he waved back before submerging again. She was so excited and watched for a while, before Timmy got bored and got out. Everyone got up, and Timmy hugged his mom and dad.

As they left, Timmy said, "Thank you, mom." After that, they walked home together and all was well again.

When they got home Timmy ran into the house while his mom and dad got out of the car. They went in without a word, and the dream ended.

m
SWINEHART
The Haitian Hero

It was a remarkably horrible day in history, and for many people, it is distinctly remembered. A man named Serge, living in a remote town called Saint-Raphaël inside of Haiti, changed the fate of one girl on this day. He was at home, painting his new kitchen table that he had built. Serge had no idea that an earthquake would be ruining his home and everything around it in a matter of seconds.

The earthquake hit and destroyed everything in its path. After it ended, he fervently wanted to help others, even though he was wincing in pain from the table that had fallen on top of him. The wet paint was all over him as well. Despite his pain, he made the gambit to leave the safety of his home and help other people in need.

Within a few minutes, a woman named Mahalia came up to him bewildered. She explained to him that her daughter, Nadia, was lost. He of course helped the frantic lady. They looked everywhere for her. At one point, they thought they'd never find her. They heard a young girl yelling for help, and Mahalia could recognize her daughter's scream anywhere. They ran to her quickly, and found that she was confined under some fallen rubble. He quickly devised a plan.

Serge decided to climb under it and just go in, ignoring the excruciating pain he was about to face. As he went in, he got numerous abrasions from the coarse rubble. He tried to conceal the pain, so Nadia wouldn't get more nervous than she already was. When he got to her, she was fatigued and dehydrated from crying and screaming. He noticed that the rubble was starting to shake. Serge now realized that he didn't have much time and needed to get her out fast. He pulled her out from under a big piece of rubble.

Suddenly, everything above them came crashing down on Serge's body. He yelled for her to run with what little energy he had left. He didn't want any more harm to come to her. Nadia ran as fast as her legs could take her. Her mother was crying and hugging her, but soon realized that the man had not made it out. This made the woman cry harder ; she couldn't believe someone lost their life to save her daughter.

Five years later, Nadia and her mother Mahalia visit Serge's grave. He was one of many brave people who lost or risked their life to save others. For this, he and many others are remembered.

ᴨ
TANAKA

John wakes up to the sound of someone shouting his name. He slowly gets out of bed and stares at his alarm clock. While his name is still being called, he squints his eyes and slowly realizes that he's late for school! It was finally apparent to him that the people shouting his name were his parents. He digs his clothes out of the closet and runs down the stairs.

Everyone at school seems surprised when they see John running in through the front door like a cheetah. He quickly goes to his locker, grabs his history book, and walks into class casually, so no one will suspect that he was almost late for school. But when he walks through the door, everyone in class stares at him with unforgivable eyes. Everyone knows! When John finally sits down in his seat, he hears a familiar voice. "What happened to you? You look very fatigued."

He peers behind him and finds out that the voice belongs to his friend, Victor. John tries to answer his question, but notices a man standing near them. He looks down at them with a sardonic smile on his face. It's their teacher.

His name is Mr. Philip. He is one of the scariest teachers in school! He loves to disconcert students and sometime even parents and other teachers. Everyone just calls him "The Eccentric One." John has never met anyone who is as brusque. Mr. Philip slowly walks up to the front of the room and starts laughing. A moment later, he finally says, "Tomorrow, one of the biggest projects will be due. If you don't write your name on it, you will get a zero and fail my class!"

John is freaking out! For this project, people needed to research one famous person who lived in the 1800s and write a ten page report on that person. He was afraid that he wouldn't be able to finish it because he procrastinated and hadn't even started on it. Victor sees his worried state and tries to reassure him, but Victor doesn't know John hadn't start his project yet. After school, John is trying to go back home in a hurry, but he is stopped by Victor, who says, "I got this cool video game that I bought. Wanna play?"

John tries to say no, but he thinks for a while and believes he could finish the project in about one hour. Then he hesitantly says yes. John somehow knew that he made a wrong choice, but playing the video game was more important to him than doing the project.

The exhilaration of the game that Victor bought was mind blowing! John thinks that the main story of the game and the graphics are amazing! John stays at Victor's house for several hours, and he finally notices that it was almost dinner. He hastily made his way home. He ran as fast as he could down the street to his house, and he was able to make it in time for dinner.

After stuffing food into his mouth, John went upstairs and was thinking what he had for homework, *The Project*. He totally forgot about the project, and now he only has two hours to do it before he goes to sleep. He needs find a way out of this! He thought and thought and thought. Finally, he gets a brilliant idea! He can trick his older sister, Julie, into doing his project for him! She is a kind hearted person, so John thought that if he made up a clever excuse that was believable, he would be able to trick his sister into doing it!

He slowly walked up to her room with a depressed face. She asks, "What happened? Are you okay?"

John replies in a remarkable way, "Could you please help me on my project that's due tomorrow? I have too much homework, so I'm not able to finish it. In English, I need to write a five page essay for the 4th time using a complicated prompt, and it is also due tomorrow! So please, PLEASE help me on the project!"

It looks like she had tears in her eyes, and she finally replies, "Don't worry, I will finish the project for you. I know how hard this project is because I had the same teacher two years ago, so just go finish your essay." John knew his sister can't resist helping because she is usually happy to help him do homework. He says thanks and slowly backs away from her room with a grin. He then goes downstairs to watch a movie with his parents on the flat screen T.V.

After watching the movie, he thinks that the movie was terrible, but it was better than doing the project. John went back upstairs and sleeps comfortably on his bed. A couple of hours pass, and Julie is still working on the project. She leaves her room to take a break and notices something odd. She sees all the movies out from the cabinet. She then asks her parents what John was doing. They said he was watching movies with them, and that is when she finally figured out that she was tricked into doing the project.

She marches right into John's room. She's furious! When John wakes up from the furious stomping, he sees his sister shredding the ten page report into tiny pieces over him. She then slams the door to his room and marches back into her room. He didn't believe his eyes, but he was glad that she didn't tear up anything else. Now he has a ten page report to write. It was already 12:00 a.m. He slowly got up and waddled to his desk.

A couple of hours had already passed, so he decided to write about Andrew Jackson because he was always interested in him. He has four more hours until school starts, and he is still on his third page. He struggled to stay awake, so some of the sentences did not make sense, but that didn't matter right now. He needed to finish the report.

The next day before going to his own class, John went to Julie's class. She sees him walk in and frowns at him, but John answers it with a grin. He walks towards her and takes the homework on her desk. Then he tears it up in front of her and leaves. He wanted revenge!

John was almost late for class again, but he managed to finish his ten page report. He was half asleep during history class, and when he got his report back, he froze. He got a big fat zero, and next to the zero there was a word that spelled out, "NAME!!!"

n
TAYLOR

"I should not be doing this," Mr. Wilson thought as he walked down the street with his reluctant new accounting partner. "I should not be doing this."

*   *   *

It was late on a Saturday night when Mr. Wilson heard a rap on his door. Knock Knock.

"Who is it?" said Mr. Wilson.

"It's Beth," said a 20 year old girl who was very smart and good looking.

He opened the door and said, "Hey, what do you need?"

"I am thinking about running a homework service. The service will be where guys pay me to help them on their homework. You will go sit at a different table to make sure the guys pay. I know I am asking a lot, but it will pay a remarkably large amount of money," Beth said with a slight grin.

"Ok, Beth; I will do it because I need the money, but we can't use my real name. Oh, I got it. I will go by Croc."

"Why Croc?" said Beth

"Because crocodiles are cool, so I want to go by Croc," said Mr. Wilson.

"Okay, that's a little weird, but thanks you're a life saver," Beth said.

*   *   *

Mr. Wilson and his partner John, a very large man who always won his fights against other men, walked into an apartment. The apartment building of the man who was not on the best terms with Mr. Wilson. John had concealed a rubber band gun in his pocket so no one could see it. He planned on using the gun against the man who had harmed Mr. Wilson.

*   *   *

It was late on a Friday night, and Mr. Wilson went up to Beth's client to ask for his payment. When the man turned his head away, Mr. Wilson got the indication that he was not going to pay. This payment was vital to him this month because he was behind on his electric bill. So Mr. Wilson asked again, a bit more harshly that time, "If you don't give me my money, I will flatten you like pizza dough." The man then quickly revealed the money because Mr. Wilson's deep voice made him sound like he could beat him up. Mr. Wilson then retrieved the money. He then took Beth from the other table and they left after saying some words that are not good for children's ears.

Later the next week, Mr. Wilson was at one of Beth's normal tutoring sessions. She was tutoring a six-foot-five middle linebacker, when, all of the sudden and for no apparent reason, the man Beth was with started and charged at Mr. Wilson. Mr. Wilson had no choice but to stand upright in his chair and jump. The man caught Mr. Wilson and started beating him until some people pulled the man off him. Mr. Wilson's world went dark.

When he woke up in the hospital, all Mr. Wilson heard was beep beep beep beep. He rolled over and saw Beth and a 7 foot 2 man sitting next to her. Talk about juxtaposition. Beth said, "This is John. He is an accountant like you, Mr. Wilson, and he is going to help you get the money and find the man who hurt you."

"Thanks, John," said Mr. Wilson.

*   *   *

As John and Mr. Wilson walked up the stairs to the apartment, John brought out his rubber band gun. They arrived at the criminal's door, and John said, "You ready?"

Mr. Wilson replied, "I was born ready."

They kicked down the door and charged in the room. The man came out of his room as if he had been summoned. It seemed as if time had slowed down for John, and the only thing he could see was the iron sights of the rubber band gun pointed right at the man who hurt his new friend, Mr. Wilson. The man threw up his hands, but that didn't matter to John. John slowly pulled the trigger and watched the rubber band fly across the room and hit the man in the nose. The man cried in agony as John came back from his trance. John and Mr. Wilson then tied the man up, got Mr. Wilson's money back, and left. Mr. Wilson decided to quit the business and become Johns new accounting partner at the local city bank.

rett
WALKER
The Art of Masonry

Standing at the front of his classroom, Mr. Wilson was waiting for his students to come in for 3rd period. He wanted to give them a new essay prompt. The students sat down obediently and were apathetic when they realized Mr. Wilson was going to give them a new task.

Mr. Wilson said, "Your prompt is to explain why Holmes decided to disguise himself as a Gypsy despite the attitude towards them at the time."

Phillip, a student, asked "Why do we have to do this?"

At the speed of light, Mr. Wilson wrenches a brick from the inventory of masonry on his shelf and nails Phillip in the eye with it.

Phillip stands upright with bewilderment on his wincing face and says, "What was that?"

The class was all laughing. Mr. Wilson then explains that it was a Brick o' Knowledge.

Phillip then asked why he threw it.

Mr. Wilson says, "It is much lighter than a Cinderblock of Reason, thus it is easier to throw."

The bell rang, and all the students left the 3rd period class.

Later in the day, students entered Mr. Wilson's class for 7th period. Mr. Wilson proposes the same essay prompt for this class, also. Then, Jimbo, a student, asked the same question as Phillip asked in the previous class. Mr. Wilson was so appalled that he grabbed a Cinderblock of Reason, and whacked Jimbo, who sat in the front row, with the block.

With a grimace, Jimbo asks, "Why did you do that?"

Mr. Wilson, fatigued from answering silly questions, smashed Jimbo over the head with a Cinderblock of Reason again.

Jimbo was no longer asking silly questions.

Phillip sat in the back of the classroom the next day, with a dingy - and sodden with blood - rag obscuring his festering eye. Everyone was pretty much silent for the duration of class.

Later that day, Jimbo came in for 7th period. His mind wasn't fully restored. He couldn't speak without stuttering, and no one paid him any attention during the class.

When Jimbo left his class, Phillip was waiting for him in the hall. They decided to converse, but Phillip was the only one really doing any talking. He explained how they could sue Mr. Wilson for child abuse.

A few days later, Mr. Wilson received an invitation to court that told him to show up on March 3rd at 12 o' clock.

A week later, Mr. Wilson walked into the courtroom at 12 o 2, so he could be fashionably late. Everyone was staring in awe when he walked in. He was wearing aviator sunglasses and a leather jacket. Mr. Wilson threw his arms behind him and two police officers pulled his leather jacket off him. He sits down, kicks his feet up on the table, pulls some hot chicken out of a fast food bag and starts eating it.

Phillip started explaining to the judge how Mr. Wilson hurled a Brick o' Knowledge at his eye. As Phillip was explaining, Mr. Wilson was tantalizing Jimbo by making a derisive grimace. Then Jimbo got up, his scathed head was partly healed, and explained how Mr. Wilson smashed him with a Cinderblock of Reason.

The judge then asked Mr. Wilson why he physically assaulted the two students' faces with masonry. Mr. Wilson explains how his act was perfectly reasonable and healthy for the students. The judge, not being able to argue with his point, ruled Mr. Wilson not guilty.

Then Mr. Wilson then yelled, "Yo, we ain't done here now. I want to sue these jokers for wastin' my time!'

The two boys turned around bleakly.

The judge responds, "I like your style, so I rule this case in Mr. Wilson's favor."

Mr. Wilson relished the moment when he received 2,000 dollars.

The two boys were sad. They walked over to Mr. Wilson and apologized for trying to sue him because he hit them with masonry.

Mr. Wilson then said, "You darn right you sorry, FOOLS!"

He then pulled some bolt cutters out of the saddle bag on his motorcycle and cut the head off of a parking meter. Then Mr. Wilson hopped on his motorcycle and rode off into the sunset.

C

WANG
The Playground

After a tedious day of CTBS practice tests, Nicholas did not look forward to the long bike ride home. He could have taken the shortcut, but that path went by the playground. In that isolated town, everyone tried to avoid it. Around the playground, there were twelve foot walls with barbed wire at the top. It was to keep people from going in. Any stupid person that got close to the playground was not expected to come back alive. The playground was in the shape of a circle that was one mile in diameter. It was very old. It was even considered old when Nicholas's great great great grandpa was a kid. No one knew what was behind the walls either because no one had the guts to go in and examine what was in there. Only Will had, but when he came out, he wouldn't tell anyone what he saw.

Will had been dared to go into the playground by Nicholas, but no one thought he would actually do it. He was in there so long that eventually his parents called the police. He finally showed up one Saturday night, but he acted like his memory had been erased. Since then, Nicholas and Will haven't spoken.

The playground had created lots of stories. The most famous one is about two twin boys that were racing around the walls of the playground. After they went around the second time, they disappeared. From that day on, when you ran near the playground, you would hear two sets of running feet behind you.

As Nicholas biked home with his friend George after school, they began to talk about the playground.

George said, "I heard that the playground is going to be torn down."

Nicholas laughed. "All that's going to do is bring more trouble."

"Well, at least we're not the ones doing it," George said

Nicholas arrived at his house, did all his homework, ate, and got ready for bed. The next day, he noticed his bike was missing. In its place was a note. It read "I have taken your bike to the playground. Come get it if you want it back in one piece." Nicholas's bike was the most precious thing he owned. He showed George the note, and they prepared to retrieve it the next day.

After twenty four hours that felt like a week, it was time to get the bike. Nicholas convinced five friends to help him retrieve his bike. Will strangely offered to help, and Nicholas was grateful for it. He showed Nicholas that he had a map of the playground. Nicholas and his friends began their walk to the playground. As the group went from the sunny day to the gloomy playground they could hear the footsteps fading behind them.

Nicholas wanted to find his bike as soon as possible so he made a plan. "We are going to split up into two groups. One goes around the inner wall clockwise, and the other group goes around counter clockwise." Nicholas said. Half an hour later, they executed the plan, then a scream was heard, and both groups assumed that it was the other one. They ran towards the scream, but everyone got separated in the process. They found each other one by one, until Will was the only one still missing.

"We need to find Will!" said George.

"We don't have time. Besides, it's getting dark," said Nicholas.

The group made it back to the entrance/exit, but it was blocked off by some bushes. Suddenly, a hum came out of the bushes and sent the group running. A huge, drone burst out of the bush. Each kid took projectiles and threw them at the machine. It was enough to scare away the robot for a short period of time. They made a run for the exit. Nicholas made sure each kid crawled through the bush and made it out. He was the last one out, but when he tried to crawl through the bush, an anonymous arm grappled his leg and tried to pull him back in. After a few moments of struggling, he was able to get free. He ran home as fast as he could, using up all his stamina.

A few weeks later at recess, Will showed up and brought Nicholas to the back of the school. He proclaimed how he was the one to steal his bike and put the note there.

He was also the one who grabbed his leg and tried to kill him. As he was saying this, he pulled a small knife out of his pocket. Nicholas quickly disarmed Will and yelled for help. Will scoffed at him then ran into the playground and was never seen again. After that day, kids would be lured into the playground just like Nicholas but they would never come back out.

r

WATERS
Spelling Bee

Kaden Knight was the smartest 15 year old at Airhawk High School in Valentine, Nebraska. He aced all of his tests, and was the top kid in his class. Kaden also had a talent with spelling. He had won every spelling bee he had competed in since the second grade. He was so good, that he was invited to compete at the National Spelling Bee! He studied nonstop for two stressful months. He read words and their definitions everywhere he went. His family was driving all the way from Nebraska to Florida just for the spelling bee, so it would be his goal to win and not let his family down.

On the day of the competition, Kaden was more nervous than he had ever been, and even though he had studied, he was worried. The drive to Florida was nerve-wracking because he realized he had greater competition at this national spelling bee than just a simple school spelling bee. As Kaden and his family walked into the large auditorium where the bee was being held, he saw just how many people he was competing against. There were around 200 other spellers that were about his age. He started to think his chance at winning the National Spelling Bee was very slim. Though it was difficult, he pushed the negative thought out of his mind and went to register as his family found their seats.

After a long introduction by an elderly man, the competition began. Several kids were in front of Kaden, which made him less tense because the more kids that were in front of him, the better chance of them getting out first. Their words weren't very challenging as they got simple singular nouns for their terms such as *government, electricity,* and *disobedient.* Only a few kids got eliminated. It was now Kaden's turn and he made his way to the microphone.

"Your word is *euouae,*" the judge spoke.

Kaden had no reaction as he thought the word was a piece of cake. "Euouae. E-u-o-u-a-e. Euouae," he responded.

"Correct!"

Kaden went back to his seat with a smile on his face because he knew he was going to do well in this spelling bee. He looked out into the silent audience and spotted his family. After a while, it was almost Kaden's turn again. Even more kids had gotten disqualified with words like *scurrilous, convenience,* and *asceticism.* Now, there were only about half of the spellers left. It was Kaden's time again as he walked to the front of the stage.

"Your word is *machiavellianism.*"

Kaden took a deep breath as he knew this was a long word to spell. "Machiavellianism. M-a-c-h-i-a-v-e-l-l-i-a-n-i-s-m. Machiavellianism." The cadence of his voice reverberated through the auditorium.

"Correct!"

The next round, even more people were disqualified with the words *onomatopoeia*, *imperturbable*, and *innocuous*. The words were getting tougher and tougher, but for Kaden, his words were oddly getting easier, which he wasn't used to. He started to lose hope about the Bee because whenever he got "easy" words, he had a fear that he would make a stupid mistake. That's why he was worried about the Bee. It was his turn, and he timidly walked towards the microphone.

"Your word is *desiccation*."

He knew this word was too easy for his liking. Hesitantly, Kaden slowly said, "Desiccation. D-e-s-i-c-uhh-c-a-t-i-o-n. Desiccation."

"Correct!"

Relieved, he went back to his seat. It was getting closer to the end, and so many spellers had been eliminated. Now, it was only Kaden and another kid named Douglas left. At this point, Kaden looked dehydrated, but he was just merely nervous. He walked to the center of the stage and was tremulous.

"Your word is *confident*."

Kaden froze. He was shaking; he couldn't think. He had heard the word several, several times before, but the pressure was on. This one word could change his whole life around. He asked for the definition and expected an elaborate one, but only got a vague two word response: "self-assured." He thought it was over. He thought he was going to lose, but right then a light bulb went off. Kaden remembered his favorite song "Boss" by Fifth Harmony.

All of a sudden Kaden sang, "C-o-n-f-i-d-e-n-t. That's me, I'm confident!" and remarkably got it right! The crowd looked amazed. It was Douglas's turn and his word was "aficionado."

His voice was hoarse as he spoke "Aficionado. A-f-f-i-c-i-o-n-a-d-o."

"I'm sorry, but that is incorrect. This makes Kaden Knight this year's National Spelling Bee winner!" the judge announced.

Douglas had no emotion as he just stood there looking disappointed.

"Wait, for real?!" Kaden asked with curiosity. The judge nodded as confirmation. He then was rewarded with $10,000 in cash. He was filled with exhilaration.

Douglas walked to him and said "Congratulations. You did an excellent job!"

"Thanks! You too!" Kaden responded.

After the competition, he received compliments from his family. They all went out to eat and relish the moment. On the long drive back to Nebraska, Kaden thought this would be a day he'd remember forever, as he listened to the song that helped him win.

eli
WHITE
Lobster Crime

"Hey there, what are you doing?" an anonymous man asked on the dock a couple feet away from me.

I replied, "Why, I was about to get some lobster until you rained on my parade."

"Well, if you don't mind, I'm going lobstering, too!" he retorted cheerfully.

"Okay, but don't catch any of my lobsters," I said, ending the conversation.

I said that because I want all the lobsters I can get. I'm a lobster lover and live on the coast of Maine. *Lobster 24/7* is my lobster boat. After that conversation, I gingerly went through my inventory and then started lobstering in the Atlantic Ocean. I didn't really have a plan for fishing; I just went out onto the considerably large sea. I didn't think much of the man who I met earlier until we crossed paths again. He yelled out, "I bet I have more lobsters than you!"

Then I shouted back, "Oh yeah? How's that?"

As I screamed that, I was pulling up a crate that was filled to the brim with over 50 lobsters! He then quickly threw a knife because he wanted more lobsters than me, which somehow cut my line, and the crate of lobsters fell down to the desolate bottom of the sea! It was the heat of the moment, and I decided to shoot the despicable man with the emergency gun in my boot. Right then, I knew I had to run away because I thought I saw something or someone in the distance. This was not how I thought my night would go. I thought it would be quiet because I had to get home to my wife and two kids. Shooting someone and making them succumb to death is gruesome just to think about. Now I have to modify my plan to catch lobsters so I don't get caught.

Later that night, I rushed back to my house to find my wife and kids. I told her what happened, and she started crying. Then after a few minutes, she replied, "Go live on my grandma's farm. It's very rural, but just act casual, and no one will notice. I'll alert her that you're coming."

I didn't take the public plane because that would be too risky. I drove all the way to Nebraska, which appeared to be the lamest state in the country. I finally pulled up to a bleak house. I knocked and said, "Hello?"

She answered, "Who is it?"

I said back, "Johnny, you're granddaughter's husband."

She then slowly walked to the door, wearing a nightgown in the middle of the day, and opened it while saying, "Honey, come in. How are you doing?"

"Good," I replied. There was a long pause. "Actually I'm not good to be honest with you, Regina. I killed a man," I said slowly, afraid she might faint.

"That's okay. I've done that many times, which you probably already know, and they still haven't caught me," she said, laughing vigorously. "You're gonna need a fake name just in case one of them police officers shows up."

"Um-" I started but never finished because Ms. Carson interrupted me.

"Great! So let's get started," she exclaimed.

I felt good about this situation. My wife's grandmother is a little on the crazy side, but she's protecting me. A couple of days passed, and no one showed up at the house. I felt great here, until Tuesday night. Something outside seemed amiss.

Ms. Carson walked into the guest bedroom where I was reading a magazine because she had no television. She whispered softly, "Why don't you tell me just what happened that night?"

I was about to rebuff her until I saw the look on her face. It was almost like she was a kid wanting something, and if she didn't get it, she was going to whine. I replied, "Okay. I was out fishing for lobsters when a guy said something like he was catching more lobsters than me, which is irrelevant. Anyways, I shot the man because he cut my line. But I destroyed the evidence by throwing the gun into the-"

A voice screamed, "Here I come, Johnny! You didn't kill me! You thought you could hide, but it wasn't good enough!"

He kicked down the front door and then came into the guest room where we were. The man was clad in old clothes with a blood stain on his right shoulder where I shot him. He yelled, "Payback!"

Right there, my heart dropped. But then I couldn't feel it because he shot me but left grandma. She got up, and when he tried to walk out, she beat him unconscious with her cane. Blood on the carpet, clothes, everywhere. She tried to come back and help me, but it was too late. I was gone.

jack
WILHITE
Lamby

Frank Peterson was a farmer in Iowa and a really good one, too. However, Frank was different than other farmers since he was a lamb farmer. The reason he raised lambs was simply because he was fascinated with their behavior. There weren't many lambs in Iowa which allowed him to be the only wool salesman in the area. Farmer Frank had a special father-child relationship with his lambs, due to the fact that they were his only friends. One day, Farmer Frank found a considerably large amount of land in Panama City, Florida online. He had always wanted to move to Florida but couldn't because he didn't want to leave his lambs behind. Farmer Frank called the landowner and received a good deal of land on the beach. He was also granted the approval of letting the lambs live there as well. Shortly after the purchase, he packed up his things and transported his lambs to the new land. Despite the curious neighbors and other difficulties, Frank still found a way to maintain the lamb farm.

After a few weeks of living on the beach, something remarkable happened that would change history. One of Farmer Frank's lambs by the name of Lamby came across a magic shell while walking on the beach. Since lambs aren't the brightest of all the animals in the world,

Lamby decided to lick the shell. As soon as he did, his whole body began to tingle in a way it never had before. Then the craziest, most significant thing to lamb-kind happened.

"What the hay just happened to me?" Lamby said. As soon as he had spoken, the other lambs began staring at him. "Whoa!" Lamby exclaimed. "Am I talking like Farmer Frank?" The shell somehow made him understand and communicate in human language. Lamby then contemplated in a cursory fashion about the reason he had received the ability to talk like Farmer Frank and other humans. Then it hit him. He realized that the tingly sensation probably came from the shell giving him this new ability. Lamby decided it would be best if he hid the shell so other lambs didn't experience the same thing. He hid the shell in the sand after digging a hole. Lamby then galloped back to Farmer Frank who was in the barn fixing a broken plow.

"Oh, hey Lamby. What's going on?" Frank said expecting a regular "baa" from the lamb.

"Farmer Frank! I licked a shell, and now I can talk like you!" Lamby replied. Farmer Frank had no idea what was going on. A lamb had just talked in human language. He didn't know what to do or if Lamby was even a lamb.

"Get out of here, you figure of witchcraft!" Frank yelled in shock. "You are no lamb of mine!" After being rejected by his own master, Lamby grew very despondent. All he felt was sheer agony. Lamby felt that he had no place anymore, so he took off for as far away as he could get from the beach farm, sobbing the whole time. Lamby just kept galloping and galloping at full speed.

After a week of traveling, only stopping to eat and drink, Lamby had reached the city of Miami, but he didn't plan on stopping. Since Miami was a large city of a modern population, people grew confused as to why there was a lamb there. When Lamby became thirsty, he decided that he would get a drink in an empty flower pot with rainwater inside. As soon as he lowered his head to drink, a rather large lady came out of an apartment building with a broom. She raised the broom to strike Lamby.

"Hey watch where you point that thing, fatty. I've had it so rough lately, and you're just making it worse. Now go back inside your apartment and get back to those donuts you've probably been eating for 20 years now," Lamby told her. The enlarged lady didn't know if it was a talking lamb in her presence that confused her or the very aggressive ways he called her fat. She ran inside, screaming. A few minutes later, an Animal Control truck pulled up to where Lamby was drinking. The lady had called them to take care of the talking lamb. An Animal Control officer hopped out of the car with a goad. He started poking Lamby.

"What the hay is wrong with you humans? Stop messing with me!" Lamby yelled. Again, a human was confused by the talking lamb. The officer went back to the truck and retrieved a huge net. Lamby just kept eyeing the officer. The officer shut the truck door and ran at the talking lamb and threw the net. Lamby was trapped. "Get me out of here!" Lamby yelled while struggling. Unlike the fat lady and Farmer Frank, the officer had an idea that would positively affect Lamby and himself. The officer called his cousin named Jimmy Fallon who had a very popular talk show. His idea was that Jimmy could include the talking lamb on the Jimmy Fallon Show so he could earn a large amount of money. Jimmy also thought it was a good idea, so he agreed to include the lamb. The officer, whose named was or Larry, released Lamby and asked him to be on the show. Lamby gladly agreed because he knew that his popularity would grow. Larry allowed Lamby to stay at his house as long as he wanted since they became good friends.

The day came when Lamby was going on the Jimmy Fallon show, and he didn't know how the world would react to his English. The show started off with Lamby, clad in his distinctive puffy wool, being introduced by Jimmy. At first, the crowd sat, stunned with confusion. However, as the night went on, Lamby was cracking jokes that made everyone laugh. The show ended up going well and boosted Lamby's popularity. Later that week, the producers of the Jimmy Fallon show gave Lamby his own talk show called *Lambylicous*. On the show, Lamby included many different celebrities, and they always either did fun activities involving modern culture or talked about what was going on in the world. No matter what Lamby and the stars did, everyone loved the show. It became the most popular show in the world that had ever existed. Everybody from New York to Oxford knew who Lamby was.

In one of his shows, Lamby featured Kanye West, and they had a rap battle. Lamby ended up winning, but one of his lines in the rap-off was "This one is for all you lovers of the Llama, you might as well be an old dead momma."

Even though that part allowed Lamby to beat Kanye in the battle, it still insulted all the llama lovers across the world. Many people grew angry at Lamby because of the rap. Another show came later that week, and the llama lovers got together in Miami to share a piece of their mind. They decided to get revenge by doing very despicable actions to the talking lamb. The angry llama lovers followed Lamby to a dark alley with an enlarged Dumpster where he went to throw away fan mail. The llama lovers took advantage of Lamby being alone by him with clubs and sheers. They shaved Lamby until he had no more wool. Lamby was left with many cuts and abrasions.

"Noooooooooooo, not my beautiful wool!" Lamby yelled, for he knew it would decrease his popularity by looking naked with many marks. After beating up Lamby, the anonymous llama lovers ran away forever, never to be seen again.

The word spread that Lamby had been jumped and shaved so people started losing interest in him and

Lambylicious, due to the fact that his festering conditions weren't so appealing. People had demeaned the lamb and his reputation. With each show, the naked lamb lost more and more viewers, eventually making him lose *Lambylicious*. Lamby had lost everything. He had lost his mansion, sports cars, and friends due to the lack of money. The poor lamb became sad since he went from having so much to so little in a quick amount of time. He ran away under a bridge, leaving his infamous self behind. Then it hit him how much he missed Farmer Frank and his lamb acquaintances back on the beach farm. With some spare money, he was able to catch a taxi back to Panama City Beach.

When he arrived at the farm, Lamby was greeted by Frank who was getting the mail.

"Farmer Frank, oh how I have missed you!" said Lamby. The two mammals embraced each other since Frank had missed him back.

"Lamby! I'm so sorry that I had rejected you. I was just in shock that a lamb was talking to me," Farmer Frank said.

"It's okay. Most people that I met did also," Lamby replied.

"I had always watched your shows and they're hilarious. I tried contacting you, but never could," Frank said. "Come on. I'll show the other lambs that you're back." Farmer Frank took him behind the barn to the pasture of sand where the other lambs were. Lamby thought the other lambs may have been mad at him for leaving, but it ended up that they had missed him as well. They gathered around Lamby, and Lamby had remembered how good it felt to be around other non-English-speaking lambs. It was a moment to never be forgotten.

It had been two days since Lamby had returned, and things were starting to get normal again. Soon it was time to graze, and Lamby noticed something shiny in the land that was reflecting the sunlight. He dug it out and realized it was the same shell he had licked before. It was the same shell that gave him the powers. It was the same shell that started it all. It was the same shell that caused so much pain. Lamby got the idea that if he licked the shell again, he would become a normal lamb. It was what he wanted. Lamby bent down and licked the shell. The same bizarre feeling pervaded his body like before. Then Lamby knew it. He was a lamb again. He was a happy lamb.

C
WILLIAMS
Dragon & Lava

Flame's majestic dragon wings were soaring through the warm summer air. He was taking his daily 1 o'clock flight. He had just crossed the long river of Hopes and Dreams when he suddenly noticed a field full of fragrant flowers. This lured him in to go and smell the roses, and so he did, or at least he was going to until he noticed a beautiful girl standing in the field picking the fragrant roses. He subtly hovered on over to say hello before he realized he needed to fix his hair, he quickly brushed it over to its usual side and made his way on over (maybe he would finally be able to make a friend. After all it had been two weeks since he had moved to Magic Island) and he hesitantly worked up the nerve to go over and introduce himself.

"Hello, Miss," said Flame as his heart fluttered at the thought of making a friend.

"Why hello, sir, what would your name be?" questioned the beautiful girl.

"Friendly, Flame Friendly," answered the exhilarated dragon.

"What a grand name; my name is Lava Lovely," replied the girl.

And so she was, Flame thought. She was a lovely girl with an amazing lava suit that showed the fiery hot magma flowing all over, gorgeous red lava flame hair, and scorching red eyes that reflected lava. After gazing at her for quite a while, Flame reluctantly asked her to lunch…to which she remarkably replied, "Of course!"

With that, they went to Burger Kingdom and chit-chatted about life and about when Flame had moved here Flame then explained that he had just moved here two weeks ago and had not yet made any friends. The thought of this made Lava Lovely sad, so she suddenly perked up and suggested an idea, "Why don't I be your friend?" she asked flirtatious tone.

"That would be fantastic! I have been wanting a new friend since I got here and now I will have a lovely one!" rejoiced Flame.

Lava then suggested they go to her volcano and play games. Flame took her up on that offer, and they hastily finished their meals at Burger Kingdom and rode on over to Lava's volcano.

When Flame and his new acquaintance landed at her customary volcano home after flying around 5 o'clock, they began contemplating what game to play outside. They decided to walk on down to the lava river of dead dreams of rebels that were mental, unpresidential, and detrimental. Lava explained the dreadful river which sparked Flame's memory of being allergic to lava. Being terrified, he said he must go as soon as possible…...but it was all too late. Flame had already burnt his tail on the inevitable lava. Realizing this, he persistently tried to run away from the lava that, of course, was invariably there. He continued to run and when he finally reached the grass area, Flame asked Lava if she had a first aid kit, and she rushed to and go get it. When she returned with the first aid kit, he applied cream and bandages to conceal the wound and make it as discreet as possible. After Flame mellowed out from the event, they decided maybe they should just hang out at Flame's man cave from now on….since neither one of them were allergic to anything there.

YI

I accidently set my dorm on fire a few days ago. It was a grease fire, and it ended up burning the whole building down. It started as a small one, but I didn't know that you're not supposed to extinguish grease fires with water. The inferno went up to the ceiling, and eventually spread to the halls. No one died, though; we're just suffering from various injuries, like third-degree burns and broken bones. My roommates are speculating that I started the fire since I'm awful at cooking and frequently burn my food. I told them that I was sleeping at the time in order to conceal the truth that I put them in the hospital with my cooking incident. Remarkably, they believed me since they were also asleep. I guess karma caught up with me, because I share my hospital room with an old lady.

Her name is Rashida, and she likes knitting and watching reality TV. She rarely talks to me. From the little conversation I've had with her, I found out that she's about to die. She said that her time on Earth is almost over, and then continued to knit. One of my classmates from Computer Engineering was recovering in the room across from me, but she passed away recently. When I asked my nurse about how she died, I received a vague answer. So, I assume it's because of how serious her injuries were. Rashida thought my classmate was an eccentric, because Vidalia was named after a type of onion, a Vidalia onion, and had vibrant pink hair. She isn't wrong though; Vidalia was a bit odd. She used to catch bugs and then release them into the classroom. Vidalia said that it calmed her down, but I don't know how having about twenty various insects fly around her for two hours calmed her down.

It's four in the morning now. I stayed up, because Rashida snores like a lumberjack. My hours of thinking made me realize that Rashida could die today, maybe right now, and no one can stop the inevitable. So, when she wakes up, I'm going to attempt to build a friendship with her. I remember her saying that she's out of touch with her family, and all of her friends are dead. I don't want her to pass away friendless. I'll probably start some casual conversation on some reality TV shows she watches a lot, assure her that the mittens she knitted are identical, and help her relish what little time she has left. The TV is just staring at me, so I turn it on to the news. I start to feel sleepy as I listen to the weatherman talk.

I woke up to a really loud crash. The sound is merely Rashida's reality TV though; she turns the volume up to max when a fight breaks out. She paid no attention to my awakening and continued to munch on her salad. I look over to my right, and a bacon and cheddar salad awaited me. I grab the food and look over to Rashida. She's staring intently at the TV, where three people are throwing glass objects and yelling scathing words at each other. The commercial break starts to play, and Rashida puts all of her attention on her salad. This is the perfect opportunity to start befriending her. I ask her how her food is. No reply from Rashida. I try to start another conversation, but she continued to ignore me. Her show starts again. It's harder than I thought it was to befriend an elderly woman. I take a bite of my salad, and then I feel something gross in my mouth. I start to gag, and when I accidentally spit out my chewed up lettuce onto my uneaten food, I see strands of hair. Upon inspection, I see that the hair is vibrant pink and very long. I shrug it off though. It's normal for me to find hair in my meals here. The cooks usually neglect to wear their hairnets. I look over to Rashida, hoping that she'll show some concern to my gagging, but she is still entranced by her show. She never pays attention to me though, so it didn't make me sad or anything.

It's around midnight now. Rashida fell asleep while knitting. I'm still awake, since Rashida snores so loudly. I ponder over life's meaning if aliens exist – but then the door opened suddenly. I go under my covers, since all of the patients have a curfew here. I leave an opening in my sheets so I can see what's happening. Some nurses walk in, and they go past me. They stop at Rashida's bed and start to move her onto a wheel chair. Rashida still slept, she pretty much sleeps through anything. Rashida and the nurses move out of the room, and curiosity pushed me out of me out of my bed and into the hallway.

They would've told Rashida ahead of time if she was having surgery, but they didn't. So she shouldn't be taken out of her room during the middle of the night. I follow the sound of the nurses' footsteps, and I eventually end up at what seems to be the lowest floor of the hospital. The nurses and Rashida enter a room hidden behind large crates. After they go in, I hurry over to the doors and look through the circular windows. Inside the room was a giant metal table, and on top of it was Rashida, strapped down with the iron cuffs built in. She was still, of course, asleep. Three surgeons walk over to the table, each holding a butcher knife, like the ones used to cut beef and other meats. One of them holds the knife above Rashida's throat, and then swiftly slices it. Blood spills over the counter. My body feels cold, and my heart is racing. I can't take my eyes off what is happening, though. The three surgeons start to disassemble Rashida, starting with taking off her head, and then removing her legs and arms. One took care of removing the flesh off her torso, another with her arms, and the other with her legs. They tore her apart as if she was livestock.

When they stopped, all that's left is her head and bones. One of the nurses, who I recognize as mine, took the flesh cut off of Rashida and put it in a cooler labeled "Pork - cut 1/17/15." To the right of the cooler was a pile of vibrant pink hair and Vidalia's head, already starting to fester. I feel gross, disgusting. All of the meat they've fed us here was human most likely. As I step back, ready to run out of this hospital, I bump into the wooden crates. They fall on top of me and make a huge ruckus. I try to get up, but my nurse, covered in blood, came out and saw me. She grabs me by my arms as I try to escape. A sharp pain shoots up my arm, and my body starts to feel numb. I look over to my arm, and a syringe, injected by my nurse, was stuck into me. My vision fades.

I wake up on the cold, metal, table they used to hold Rashida. My arms and legs are cuffed down, and my body is numb. The scent of blood fills my lungs. A surgeon hovers over me, and readies his knife over my throat. I try to shout for help, but I see the knife come down, and I slowly lose my breath. My vision fades to white.

appendix
THE COVERS

Just as with the rest of this book, the front and back covers were a collaborative effort. Students suggested individual ideas that then faced off against each other two at a time until there were only three left for the front and three left for the back. Consider it an artistic variation of March Madness…if there were two winners.

The winner for the front? Rett Walker.

Once the rough idea for the front was established, other students tried their hand at bringing it to life.

Aaron Brewer's entry (originally in color).

B. Golden's entry.

A. Rutherford's entry.

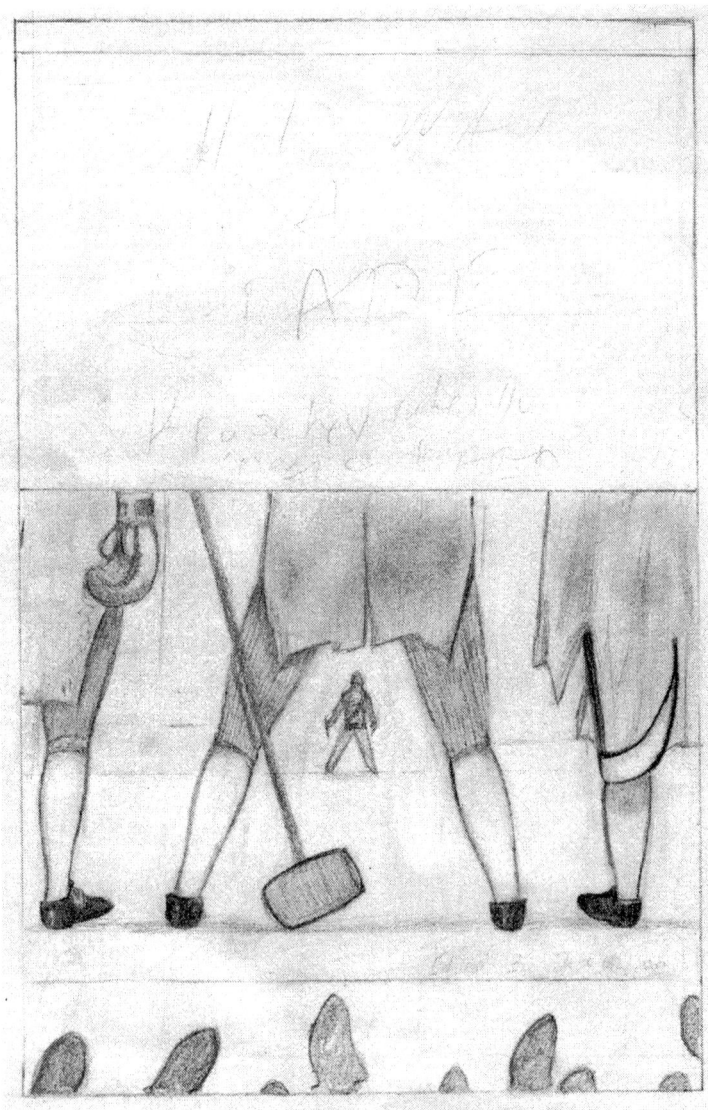

After A. Rutherford's won, Aaron Brewer tried his hand at coloring it, but Rutherford's own coloring won the day. A little digital tweakage later, and the cover became what it is now.

In terms of the back, it was T. Hatch's idea that won.

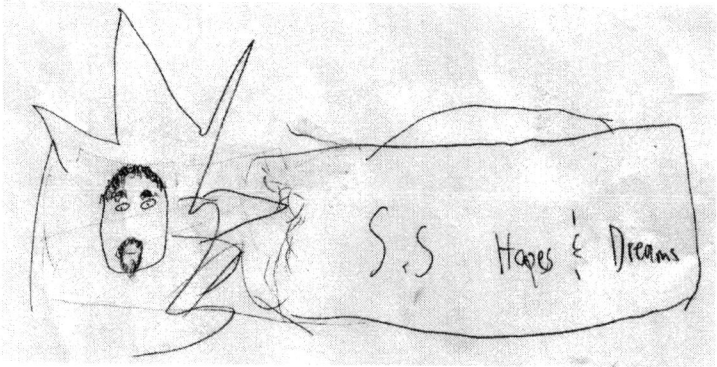

This idea, of a ship called the S.S. Hopes & Dreams crashing into an iceberg featuring a goatee and glasses, resulted in a few different interpretations.

Aaron Brewer's entry (originally in color).

B. Golden's entry.

Octavia N. Martin's entry (originally in color).

S. Yi's entry.

S. Yi's entry won after a close battle. A few different students tried coloring Yi's entry, but B. Golden and Aaron Brewer were both beat out by Yi's own coloring, which is by and large what can be seen on the back of the book now.

41496169R00186

Made in the USA
Lexington, KY
15 May 2015